IN YOUR FACE

IN YOUR FACE

FACE

A CARTOONIST AT WORK

DOUG MARLETTE

Houghton Mifflin Company · Boston · 1991

For information about permission to reproduce selections from this book, write to Permissions,
Houghton Mifflin Company, 2 Park Street, Boston, Massachusetts 02108.

Library of Congress Cataloging-in-Publication Data

Marlette, Doug, date.
In your face : a cartoonist at work / Doug Marlette.
       p.   cm.
ISBN 0-395-60236-X. — ISBN 0-395-56274-0 (pbk.)
1. Marlette, Doug, 1949- — Psychology.   2. American wit and
         humor, Pictorial.   I . Title.
            NC1429.M4215A2   1991
        741.5'092 — dc20   91-19925
                                CIP

Book design by Anne Chalmers

Printed in the United States of America

HAD   10 9 8 7 6 5 4 3 2 1

FOR MY WIFE, MELINDA,
AND OUR FIRSTBORN, JACKSON,
WITH LOVE, HIGH FIVES, AND GRATITUDE

CONTENTS

INTRODUCTION

If Elvis had drawn, he would have drawn cartoons.

Good cartoons are like visual rock and roll. They hit you primitively and emotionally, turning you every which way but loose. There is something wild and untamed about the best of them, raw and vaguely threatening, like Little Richard or Jerry Lee Lewis. Just as rock and roll made the disapproving parents of the fifties raise their eyebrows and call it jungle music, cartoons are jungle art to the guardians of today's journalistic decorum. Unruly, impertinent, and bristling with attitude, they just won't mind.

That's why the fastidious *New York Times* refuses to run them. As *Times* editor Max Frankel said, sitting across from me at the Pulitzer Prize ceremonies, "The problem with cartoons is you can't edit them." Exactly. They're out of control and do not willingly serve as handmaidens to finely tuned and delicately calibrated editorial policies. They're a "problem" for control freaks and for the editors at the *Times*, which is precisely the source of the cartoon's power and its glory.

A cartoon cannot say "on the other hand," and it cannot be defended with logic. It is a frontal assault, a slam dunk, a cluster bomb. Journalism is about fairness, objectivity, factuality; cartoons use unfairness, subjectivity, and the distortion of facts to get at truths that are greater than the sum of the facts. Good cartoonists are also the point men for the First Amendment, testing

VISUAL ROCK 'N' ROLL

the boundaries of free speech. If they are doing their job, their hate mail runneth over.

Who can ever forget David Levine's caricature of Lyndon Johnson at the height of the Vietnam War, pulling up his shirt to show us his scar: a map of Vietnam. That single image stays with us long after the thundering editorials about the war have wrapped fish and lined bird cages. Bill Mauldin's image of a bereaved and weeping Lincoln Memorial unforgettably captured a nation's grief over President Kennedy's assassination. Herblock's drawing of Richard Nixon emerging from a sewer defined the president in a way that neither we nor Nixon can ever shake.

Editorial cartooning and comic strips are enjoying a renaissance. The talent, competition, and professional standards have never been higher. Having participated in and watched the growing impact and popularity of cartooning from the inside, I'm ready to let America in on some of the secrets of its own pop soul. *In Your Face* is not an overview of the profession, nor is it a how-to guide. I am not a historian or a teacher. Cartoons and their creators are as individual as thumbprints, and I could never speak for other cartoonists, even if I wanted to. This book is an anecdotal exploration of the world of the cartoonist; it is as personal as my own squiggly lines.

I draw editorial cartoons and a strip called "Kudzu" (in the trade I'm known as a double-dipper), so I can talk about the vicissitudes of both quirky callings. I try to illuminate with drawings, sketches, rough drafts, editorial cartoons, and comic strips, as well as words, the workings of the mind of a cartoonist. Or as my comic-strip preacher, Reverend Will B. Dunn, might put it, I hope to "unscrew the unscrutable."

IN YOUR FACE

A DAY IN THE LIFE OF A CARTOON

5 A.M.

IDRAW ON DEADLINE, so I can't sit around waiting for inspiration to strike. It doesn't always show up on schedule, so I have to stalk that sucker, hunt it down and ambush it. We wrestle and grapple until I force it, like Jacob's angel in the Old Testament, to bless me. I can't go home until I pin the son of a bitch. And I do this every day.

At 5:00 A.M. my alarm goes off, and I make my way out of the bedroom and down the hall. Outside it's pitch dark. Unless my four-year-old's Tinker Toys were left in the hallway the night before, I can get there pretty well for a left-handed person, without waking my wife and son.

In the shower, I make myself go over last night's top news stories, the local murders, rapes, and ambulance chasers in addition to the latest news from the war in the Persian Gulf. My adrenalin starts pumping.

Out of the shower, shaved and dressed, I head upstairs to make coffee. It's 5:30, and *New York Newsday*, the paper I work for, and the *New York Times* are out on our stoop.

Newsday has the best coverage of the city, so I read it first. No other paper can touch it for all-around thoroughness and high-quality journalism. The *Times* is stuffier, but it does its national and international thing better than the rest. If the newspapers aren't there, I hit CNN's "Headline News," popcorn for news and political junkies. National Public Radio's "Morning Edition" and "All Things Considered" are also on my diet.

The coffee has the same effect on my insides as the shower has on my outsides. All systems are humming.

Before I troll for today's topic I check my cartoon in *Newsday* to make sure it reproduced well — no lines dropped out or crosshatches bleeding. I also want to see if it works as well in the cold, unforgiving light of dawn as I thought it did yesterday. All the talk of terrorism since the war started has really hit New York City.

"RELAX, DEAR !... HE'S NOT A TERRORIST—HE'S JUST A MUGGER!"

When I see my drawing surrounded by type and columns it looks different than it did on the drawing board — more official. Today I get the same thrill seeing my work, feeling newsprint, smelling the ink, as I did when I was sixteen years old and first had a drawing printed in the local paper. It's one of journalism's primal pleasures.

I start reading the newspapers with a scavenger's eye. Today I am in luck. I have many worthy targets. For starters, the Soviet tanks in Lithuania and Gorbachev's seeming pullback from the promise of *perestroika* are pretty upsetting.

But other stories also register on my Richter scale of outrage. The Persian Gulf war is a wellspring of topics. Since the beginning of the war a few weeks ago, the initial rush of giddy anxiety has subsided, but every day it offers up any number of cartoon opportunities. Today we have the continuing Scud attacks on Israel, reaction to Saddam Hussein's intentional fouling of the environment with oil spills, and the Pentagon's tight control of the press and coverage of the war. All of this against the backdrop of the most massive air assault in history and the inevitability of a bloody ground war.

Locally the abysmal state of the city's finances and Mayor

Dinkins's proposed real estate tax are worth commenting on, but yesterday's terrorism cartoon had a New York slant, and I like to follow a local cartoon with a national or international one. The city's fiscal problems will be around for some time.

The war stories are tougher to pass on. The sad truth is that war is as much a boon for cartoonists as it is for arms merchants. I could draw on the war every day and never run out of material. Other big stories get pushed to the back burner during such national cataclysms. Now it's time to focus on something else. If I don't hit the Baltic situation today, I may lose the opening.

Timing is everything in cartooning. News stories are like waves breaking over the public's consciousness. Cartoonists are the surfers, trying to catch the issue just as it crests, not too soon but not too late. Timing is more critical in New York City than in smaller cities like Charlotte or Atlanta, where I worked before. New York has a faster pace, and New Yorkers have an attention span of nanoseconds. In Charlotte, if the school superintendent died I could wait a day to draw an obit cartoon; in New York it takes only a day for my audience to grieve and move on to something else.

Cartoonists are only as good as our raw material. Hot topics make hot cartoons, and a slow period will show up in our work too. When readers or colleagues tell me, "You've really been on a roll lately!" I know it has as much to do with that week's news as it does with my own wit and imagination.

I like cartoons that make me laugh out loud or gag on my Wheaties or spit out my cappuccino. I like cartoons that grab me by the collar, slap me around, and send me on my way. They should make me feel something — amusement, sadness, outrage, something. When I sit down at my drawing board I try to knock my own socks off. If I don't feel any emotion, I can't expect readers to feel anything either — much less hang the cartoon on their refrigerator.

I feel something about glasnost crumbling. Today the sound of tanks rolling into Vilnius, Gorbachev's silence, and the rationalizations of Kremlin hardliners seem louder even than the air raid sirens, the Pentagon press briefings, and the rumbling of B-52s in the Persian Gulf. Before the fall of communism in Eastern Europe, such an event

WHEN I SIT DOWN AT THE DRAWING BOARD I TRY TO KNOCK MY SOCKS OFF might have brought us to the brink of nuclear confrontation.

It's 6:45 A.M. I've toasted an English muffin, and I have a target for today's cartoon. It's time to grab my coat and head to work.

I split my days between the *Newsday* office in Manhattan, where I draw the political cartoon in the morning, and my studio at home, where I draw a comic strip in the afternoons. I guess I could draw them both at home, but I like going to the office to do the political cartoons; the energy and excitement of the newsroom, where breaking news is coming in all the time, are stimulating. I feel closer to the pulse of events there, and I enjoy being around other journalists.

As the cab bounces along the potholed streets, I finish reading the features section of the newspaper. An ad for a new movie called *Sleeping with the Enemy* catches my eye. Maybe there's a cartoon in it. Jordan's King Hussein and Saddam Hussein "sleeping with the enemy"? . . . Naaah . . . too much of a stretch. Movie ads can make good cartoons if they fit the topic and if the analogy is natural. The ad for the movie *Lambada, the Forbidden Dance* showed a young man in tight pants and a girl in a skimpy dress dancing lasciviously. For weeks the papers had been covering the arrival of the dance in this country, and instantly there was an exploitation movie. I used the Forbidden Dance

in a cartoon. The couple could have been East and West Germany doing the "Gestapa," but I settled on Israelis and Palestinians dancing the forbidden "Shalombada." I tear out the *Sleeping with the Enemy* ad and put it in my coat pocket. There's got to be something there.

As we cover the last few blocks I noodle the Lithuanian crisis. The Soviet Union is in big trouble. Schevardnadze recently resigned. Is Gorbachev caving in to the hard-liners? A few weeks ago, when Gorbachev won the Nobel Prize, I drew Soviet citizens standing in a bread line, one saying "Gorbachev won the Nobel Prize. Pass it on." Maybe I should focus on the change in Gorbachev.

"GORBACHEV WON THE NOBEL PRIZE—PASS IT ON!"

I pick up another cup of coffee from the deli downstairs and greet the security guard. As usual, nobody is stirring when I reach the office at 7:15. I'm pretty much the only one here until 9:30. Like an empty football stadium, an empty newsroom doesn't feel quite right.

My office is in a corner of the Editorial Page/Viewpoints suite. In one corner is a white contemporary-design adjustable drawing table, its board tilted at a slight angle. I sit on a high swivel chair; a white taboret to the left holds my drawing utensils. There is a sink for cleaning pens and brushes, a computer work station, and an office-type desk. I also have a light box, a copier, and my own fax machine.

As I unlock my office door the phone is ringing. Odd. Nobody calls this early.

"*New York Newsday*," I answer.

"Mr. Marlette?" Oh, no. It's Mrs. Mackey, the abortion lady. Why is she calling this early?

"Do you know how many unborn babies died in America last year?" Mrs. Mackey has been writing and calling me steadily ever since I drew an anti–death penalty cartoon years ago. She sends me literature and leaflets to persuade me to do pro-life cartoons.

"Good morning, Mrs. Mackey," I sigh.

"Mr. Marlette," she begins, in a soft, whispery voice that is meant to ooze Christian charity and patience but is actually pushy, insistent, and much like a fork on a blackboard. I have become Mrs. Mackey's personal responsibility. Her mission, for which she will no doubt reap rewards in paradise, is to convert the wayward cartoonist or at least force him to use one of her cartoon ideas.

"Do you take ideas for cartoons?" she asks, even though she already knows the answer.

"No, ma'am," I explain once again, trying to get her off the phone, "I have a policy. I make them up myself."

She launches into it anyway. "I was washing the dishes when it hit me out of the blue. Why don't you draw this pile of —"

"Mrs. Mackey," I interrupt, "I don't take cartoon ideas. You're wasting your time."

"No, see . . . you have this pile of fetuses, see —"

"Mrs. Mackey, I told you," I interrupt again. "I'll be happy to listen to your ideas later on today, but right now I'm on deadline!"

People seem to get seized with cartoon ideas, like fits or demons, and feel they just have to get them off their chests. This happens to most folks only once in a blue moon, but Mrs. Mackey seems to be struck every few seconds. I warn people who call in with ideas that I like to draw my own, but I'll be happy to listen to theirs. This usually satisfies, but experience has taught me that Mrs. Mackey will go on forever if I let her.

YOU DRAW *BUSH* AS THE *LONE RANGER*, SEE!... AND... AND... CONGRESS IS *TONTO*, SEE!... AND... UH... THIS WAGON TRAIN IS THE *DEFICIT*... AND YOU HAVE *BUSH* SAYING TO *TONTO*...

OCCASIONALLY A READER GETS "POSSESSED" BY A CARTOON IDEA AND IT'S MY JOB TO EXORCISE IT

"Did you get the materials I sent you?" she asks.

"Uh . . . Yes, ma'am." She's referring to a pile of pamphlets that came in the mail yesterday and are buried somewhere on my desk. Now I know who sent them.

"Did you read them?" She never lets up.

"Okay. I'm on deadline, Mrs. Mackey —"

"Just listen to this idea. On one side you have this pile of dead fetuses —"

"Not right now, Mrs. Mackey. I've gotta go!"

"And on the other side you've got a pile of corpses —"

"I'm hanging up now, Mrs. Mackey. Goodbye."

As I take off my coat I realize I should have let her finish exorcising her cartoon idea.

My actual deadline does not bear down until 6:00 this evening, but I like to finish by noon or so. This self-imposed early deadline allows me to shift gears in the middle of the day if necessary. For instance, when the Oliver North verdict came in late in the afternoon, I quickly faxed a cartoon from my home to the office in time for the early editions. Also, if someone in the head office has a problem with what I've drawn we can discuss it and I can adjust or draw another one. It's best not to argue with editors when you're under deadline pressure Also, finishing early gives me the rest of the day to work on my comic strip.

I sit down on the couch with a felt-tip marker and yellow legal pad and begin doodling. When I was twenty-two years old and first had to meet a daily deadline, it took me four hours or more to think of an idea and another four hours to draw it. I tried to get the idea by lunch, then I'd draw all afternoon right up to deadline. Sometimes I didn't find an idea until 5:00 P.M. Fortunately those days are past. It is hard to get worse at something if you practice.

At times, coming up with the idea for a cartoon is like sweating internal organs out through my pores. Mental constipation. Beads of blood pop out on my forehead. Nothing gets off the ground. Nothing punches my ticket. The captions seem clunky, they drone on and on . . . wadda, wadda, wadda . . . But I stay with it. I come back at the idea from a different angle. Sometimes I look at old cartoons to jump-start my engine. Something will come. It's like rubbing two sticks together — sooner or later a spark will catch. Amoebas divide, squirrels store nuts for the winter, and I make up cartoon ideas. It does happen.

Today my mission is strong. Soviet tanks in Lithuania are big news. I sketch and scribble on my yellow legal pad, jotting down key words or phrases . . . glasnost, *perestroika* . . . drawing the onion-domed Kremlin, Soviet tanks, Gorbachev. What if the Soviets go back to being their old nasty selves? With the Persian Gulf war sapping all our military might who's minding the store? I come up with an image of the White House with the Kremlin's onion domes on top and a balloon saying, "NATO had disarmed, we were tied up in the Persian Gulf, then Lithuania fell, then Latvia."

Hmmm. Possible, but not the point I want to make today. I want to focus on Gorbachev and his apparent betrayal of glasnost. I begin searching for ways to depict Gorby's turn-around. I start with his face. His bald head could look like a missile . . . His birthmark! . . . What if I draw it as Lithuania? . . . He's acting like Stalin . . . What if he slowly metamorphoses into Stalin . . . the return of Stalin . . . maybe a movie poster, "The Return of Stalin." I free-associate to "The Return of

FrankenStalin." That works, but there's more here . . .

The phone rings again.

"*New York Newsday.*"

"I'll be praying for you, Mr. Marlette."

"Thank you, Mrs. Mackey, but I have to get back to work."

"I'm putting you on my prayer list . . ."

"Fine," I say. I have had this honor bestowed upon me before. It is hard, I have noted, to distinguish between Mrs. Mackey's prayer list and her shit list.

"On one side you have a pile of fetuses —"

"Later, Mrs. Mackey. Call back later in the day and I'll listen to your idea. Goodbye."

Back to the couch and the Gorbachev idea. FrankenStalin works, but maybe another day. What about America's relationship to Gorbachev? . . . I mean, two years ago we were going to canonize him! Back then I drew him on Mt. Rushmore and guest-hosting the Tonight Show! . . . What happened? He changed. He's not what he seemed . . . We're like disillusioned lovers. He's more brutal than we thought . . . I think of marriage counselors . . . wife beaters . . . wait! . . . He's a sado-masochist . . .

Suddenly, I see Gorbachev in leather with a whip or chains.

I sketch him that way, but is he the husband or the wife? America is Uncle Sam . . . no, it's funnier if Gorby's a man in leather drag. So how about America as Lady Liberty? I sketch Gorby sitting in a marriage counselor's office next to Miss Liberty. Gorby, decked out in leather corset, fishnet stockings, and boots, is holding a cat-o'-nine tails. The doctor stares impassively as Liberty says, "He's changed, Doc. He's not the man I married!"

That's it! But wait, I need to tinker with the caption. Make it "Gorby's changed . . ." If I've got him in women's garb, he may need more identification than his birthmark and bald head, but I solve that by naming him in the caption. "He's not the man I fell in love with." Got it. It's 8:05 A.M. and I know what will fill the hole tomorrow.

Usually after I get my idea I take a little break and check my mail. Today there are a few letters. No packages. During the Imelda Marcos trial, Imelda's fondness for shoes prompted me to draw a big Odor Eaters truck parked outside the courthouse. The company liked the drawing and sent me an Odor Eaters T-shirt and a free sample. When you draw a product in a cartoon the manufacturers sometimes send you a sample of the product. Every chance I get I put a Mercedes Benz in my cartoons, but so far, nothing.

I also get letters from aspiring cartoonists. "I am 11 years old and like your cartoons very much," one reads. "Would you please send me a drawing and your autograph on the enclosed 3 x 5 card?" I always answer these letters because I remember how hard it was to get encouragement for cartooning when I was a kid. I quickly sketch George Bush saying, "Read my lips, Billy Fentress, keep drawing!" I address it "To Billy, a fellow cartoonist."

Leona Helmsley's attorney wants the original of a drawing I did of Leona as the Wicked Witch in a puddle in the courtroom crying, "I'm melting!" And this guy's on *her* side.

Uh-oh. Here's some hate mail. I can tell even before I open it. The writing on the envelope is a scrawl and there's no return address. Rarely do the vitriolic spewers of venom give their name or address. These people are not known for their courage. This one isn't even a letter, just a cartoon I drew of a high school principal behind a counter reading "Condoms 'R' Us" and a passing male student saying to another, "Remember when we used to hate homework?" Expletives have been scrawled across the page. Nice. And what's this in the envelope? A condom.

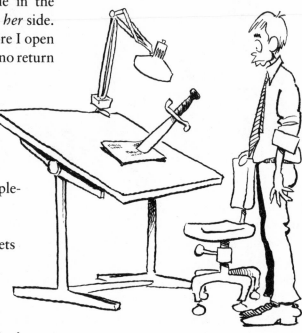

I start clearing a space on my drawing board (it gets cluttered faster than a cartoonist's mind). I throw out the reference materials that have piled up over the last few days — faxes of photos of automatic assault weapons and taxicabs and New York cityscapes that I used yesterday for this morning's cartoon. I save the pictures of the state capitol and city hall for future reference.

YOU LEARN TO RECOGNIZE HATE MAIL EVEN BEFORE YOU OPEN IT

Often before I draw something I do some research. If I'm caricaturing a politician, like the mayor or a senator, or drawing the Marlboro logo or the CBS emblem, I ask the newspaper's reference library to send me photos from their files. Sometimes I find what I need — the Japanese flag, say, or a picture of Teddy Roosevelt or the Wright brothers' plane — in encyclopedias or other reference books in the library. Reference librarians get a real chuckle from my strange requests.

Over the years I've collected my own reference books — on clothing of different eras, the monuments and buildings of Washington, New York, and Moscow, and photo stills from movies like *The Wizard of Oz*. Sometimes I call on *Bartlett's Familiar Quotations* for a famous saying or use the thesaurus or rhyming dictionary to parody a song.

At 8:15 the phone rings again. If it's not Mrs. Mackey, it must be my wife. Nobody in the city starts work until 9:30 or 10:00.

"*New York Newsday*," I answer. It's not Mrs. Mackey. Nor is it my wife.

"Is Martelle there?" It's a male voice. It sounds belligerent.

"Who?"

"Martelle. The one who drew this cartoon in the paper this morning.

"You mean Marlette?"

"Yeah. Let me speak to Marlette." Here we go.

"Speaking."

"Are you the one who drew this cartoon on terrorism?"

"Yes, I did," I recklessly admit.

"What did it mean?" he asks coyly.

"What did you think it meant?" I counter, a tactic I have learned from years of dealing with hostile phone calls.

"I think it means you're a nigger lover!"

"Excuse me?"

"Why didn't you make the mugger a nigger?"

"What?"

"You heard me!" he rails. "You and your goddam newspaper are nothing but nigger lovers. That's why you supported Dinkins, 'cause you're all a bunch of Jews!"

"Actually, I was raised Southern Baptist."

"This city can stand some law and order or there won't be no city!" the caller philosophizes.

"Sir, why don't you write down these opinions in a letter to the editor?"

"Kiss my ass!" he explains.

"I'm sorry you feel that way —"

Click!

Back to my drawing board. It's slanted so I don't have to hunch over like Quasimodo but close enough to horizontal that things like indelible India ink don't slide off. Two adjustable lamps, each with fluorescent and incandescent bulbs, loom up from either corner over the drawing board like the eyes of an alien from outer space. The incandescent light seems to cancel out the weird static blue glow of the fluorescent. My drawing area has the brightness tinged with giddy expectation of a Broadway spotlight. A drum roll sounds every time I sit down to draw.

Along with the stray papers and mail, pencils, felt-tip markers, and brushes, I keep a T-square and an electric pencil sharpener on the board. My favorite felt-tip pen (a Niji extra fine point because it doesn't smear) is for lettering captions and signing my name.

On a large rectangular piece of two-ply paper, I rule the borders to a standard size. My original drawing is twice the size of what appears in the newspaper. The engraving department photographs and reduces the original to the right size for printing. The larger original size gives me more space to roam around in, and I find that the reduction refines the drawing. Most cartoonists draw larger than their drawings are printed.

I use a blue pencil to sketch a rough layout of the marriage counselor's office. The doctor and Miss Liberty are stock characters right out of central casting in a stock situation. The

composition and set design are simple and straightforward. Sometimes I have to try out several arrangements to see which works best. Today I don't have to.

Composition — the arrangement of elements in a drawing — determines what the eye sees and when. The composition tells a story, emphasizing one aspect visually and playing down another. Working somewhat like a film director, a cartoonist decides whether to show the action in a close-up, a medium or long shot, from a bird's-eye or worm's-eye view, or straight on. The perspective provides a specific emotional weight, so it's important to pick the right one for the idea.

A worm's-eye view, looking up from ground level, for instance, qives a scene a stark, looming, dramatic quality that emphasizes the magnitude of figures, objects, or buildings. You can make a South American dictator look even more sinister or give a mundane object like a salt shaker a majestic presence.

A straight-on, eye-level view tends to be static. With the bird's eye view, looking down on a scene, you can show more and lend the drawing objectivity and emotional distance.

The camera angle is important, as is the decision about how much or how little of a scene to show. If a character's facial reaction is the focus of the humor, I'm not going to draw a panorama that obscures facial detail. I try to find the scale that puts the idea across most clearly. Ultimately I try to remember that composition is about communicating the idea. If the drawing gets in the way of the idea, it has failed.

I usually put the speaker on the left because in our culture

TRACING PAPER LETS ME MOVE THINGS AROUND IN THE DRAWING

the eye moves from left to right. In today's drawing the speaker, Miss Liberty, is in the center, but the visual punch, Gorbachev in leather drag, is on the right.

I put the caption at the bottom. Some cartoonists always put it at the bottom, others always at the top. Recently some have opted to use comic strip–type balloons, a convention of the earliest social commentary cartoons, like those of James Gillray or Currier and Ives. I handle captions in various ways, but in this particular drawing it seems best to have the caption at the bottom to keep the focus on the faces of the three figures.

I use tracing paper so I can move things around in the drawing. If the figures are too close together or the perspective is off, I lay on another sheet of tracing paper and correct it. The drawing process is like focusing a camera lens; with each step, each refinement of the previous rough, I get closer and closer to the effect I'm after.

When I've solved all the drawing problems in blue pencil, I go back over the final sheet of tracing paper with lead pencil to firm up the drawing and put in more detail. I might strengthen the expressions of the marriage counselor or Gorby or Liberty. Then, with another piece of tracing paper and a felt-tip pen, I consolidate the drawing further into a rough finished form while trying to keep a loose quality in the drawing. There's always the danger in going over the same image several times of tightening it up so much you kill the spontaneity.

Now I'm ready to transfer the image onto Strathmore bristol board, a heavy-duty, high-quality drawing paper. I lay the bristol board over the tracing paper rough and put the two sheets over the light box. This technique allows me to ink directly on the bristol board with a Winsor and Newton #2 watercolor brush and India ink instead of cleaning up pencil marks with erasures that might lighten the ink lines on the drawing. After I transfer the basic outline onto the bristol board I can move away from the light box and fill in blacks and shade the drawing.

I want the figure of Gorby to stand out, so I fill in the black of his leather outfit and boots. Sometimes I use shadow or crosshatching in the background of a scene to make the figures pop into the foreground, but today it looks as if the natural blacks in the design will direct the eye and weight the drawing properly; it won't need any background blacks.

I am well into my drawing by the time the others start to

" GORBY'S CHANGED—HE'S NOT THE MAN I FELL IN LOVE WITH! "

arrive. I am inking the drawing, paying attention to Gorbachev's expression and eye makeup when the phone rings.

"*New York Newsday.*" I have learned over the years to answer the phone with the name of the paper instead of "Marlette" or anything more personal that might encourage all the kooks and crackpots. This gives me a little longer to decide whether to identify myself at all.

As it turns out, this is not your routine kook or crackpot. It is my editor.

"Doug? . . . Jim. How's it going?"

"Fine . . . I have something on Gorbachev tomorrow."

"Good . . . we're writing a lead editorial on the Baltic situation, too."

Jim Klurfeld is a terrific editorial page editor who likes strong cartoons, especially when the cartoon and the editorial complement each other. Still, there is no pressure or design to have them correspond. Like a columnist, I function independently; the cartoons are not tied in to anything else on the editorial page.

"I'm going to be in meetings all day out here in Long Island and I'll be in Washington the rest of the week. I'll be in the city on Monday. If you need me, Eileen knows how to reach me."

"Okay. I'll be faxing this drawing over in a few minutes." Jim is the editor who approves my cartoon before it goes in the paper.

I finish the Gorby cartoon before noon, make a reduced copy of the drawing, and fax it out to our Long Island office. The original is sent in a mailing flat by the two o'clock courier out to the Melville plant, where the engraving department processes it to run in the paper.

My secretary and I handle mail and make sure the newspapers on my list of syndicate clients are getting what they need. I look at my watch; if I leave now I can have lunch with my wife and son and start drawing my comic strip by 2:00 P.M. Just as I get my coat on, the phone rings again.

"*New York Newsday,*" I answer.

"You've got a pile of dead unborn babies on the left and on the right a pile of dead bodies. Over the babies it says New York City, 1990. Over the bodies it reads Auschwitz, 1939. The caption says 'Progress?' with a question mark."

"Not bad, Mrs. Mackey. I've never seen this whimsical side of you before."

"Do you like my idea?"

"You should be concerned. You're starting to think like a cartoonist."

"Will you use it?"

"No ma'am, I didn't say that. I just said 'Not bad.' You're thinking like a cartoonist."

"Do you know how many unborn babies died in New York City last year?"

"Goodbye, Mrs. Mackey."

PORTRAIT OF THE CARTOONIST AS A YOUNG MAN

WHERE I GREW UP, artists were rarer than Jews or Catholics. Nobody I knew drew pictures for a living. My kinfolks were mill workers, cotton and tobacco farmers, auto mechanics, and waitresses. Culture was something the veterinarian scraped off the cow's tongue to check for hoof-and-mouth disease. Art was sad-faced clowns and black velvet Jesuses. We moved around a lot, and some of the places were so backward even the Episcopalians handled snakes.

When I began putting pencil to paper, drawing things as fast as lightning bolts from my fingertips, my parents didn't know what to do with me. When I was three years old and swore I saw monster faces in the floral wallpaper, they just shook their heads and said, "That boy sure has an imagination!" When I wouldn't go into my grandmother's bedroom because I believed a dead body was in her cedar chest, they rolled their eyes. "He sure has an imagination!" I sometimes made up my own endings to fairy tales and added lines to nursery rhymes. That always got them. "He sure has an imagination!"

But when my Crayolas started scrawling battleships and jet bombers all over our new refrigerator, my imagination began to get on their nerves. By the time I was five years old, I had discovered I could copy my favorite characters from the funny papers. Lying on the floor, pencil or crayon in hand, I stared at the newspaper ads

HE CERTAINLY HAS AN IMAGINATION!

for "The Mickey Mouse Club" TV show. Then meticulously I copied Mickey: one large circle for his head, two smaller circles on each side for the ears, a small circle in the middle for the nose, and so on. Soon I could reproduce Mickey or Donald Duck or Popeye without copying.

Some children memorize nursery rhymes or jingles from TV commercials; for me, it was the sweeps and curves, squints and clefts of Popeye and friends. This made me a very popular first-grader. My classmates gave me desserts and marbles for drawing personalized Donald Ducks. I was

instantly in business. One day during recess I drew a gigantic forty-foot Popeye on the playground. My teacher gathered the class around to look at it. I shucksed and pshawed and dug my toe into the dirt as everybody oohed and aahed. They didn't exactly hoist me onto their shoulders, march me around the playground, and name a building after me, but they might as well have.

My first report card said, "Although Douglas has a tendency to visit with his neighbors during naptime, he excels in art." I was doodling and coudn't keep my mouth shut about what was going on around me — already the makings of a political cartoonist.

My second-grade teacher encouraged my parents to enroll me in weekend art classes, so early one Saturday morning I found myself walking into a studio. Several easels were set up with fresh watercolor paper and poster paints, and we were given smocks to wear. This was definitely more serious than my crayons and newsprint, and not at all like lying on the floor to create my masterpieces.

"Now, children," the teacher said solemnly, gesturing to the glorious sunlit garden of trees, flowers, and shrubbery just outside, "I want you to paint what you see."

I looked out the window and studied the landscape, glanced back down at my fresh clean watercolor paper and paints, looked out the window again, took brush in hand, and quickly drew a perfect Popeye.

Not long after that, I had my first encounter with the "Peanuts" cartoons — Charlie Brown, Snoopy, Lucy, Linus, and Schroeder; I was bowled over. The characters were so real and alive. It was magic that such simple lines, ink on paper, could create real characters with personality and expressions. My love affair with the comics spread from "Peanuts" to "Miss Peach" to "B.C." I read them all: the adventure strips, like "Steve Canyon" and "Dick Tracy"; the satirical "Li'l Abner"; the soap operas such as "Mary Worth," "The Heart of Juliet Jones," and "Mary Perkins, On Stage." When I grew up I wanted to draw L'il Abner and marry Mary Perkins.

I could count on the comics. They were there every day, right where I had left off the day before. I learned the comic strip vocabulary, the *zot*s and *gasp*s as well as the visual shorthand. It was like owning a secret decoder ring. If you don't know that the speaker is connected to the dialogue balloons by little pointers, that diminishing bubbles mean the character is thinking, that a jagged-edge dialogue balloon means the character is talking loudly, excitedly, that smoke rising from a head signifies rage, and that a random series of exclamation points, curlicues, pound signs, and stars is obscene language, you're lost.

From the beginning I knew that someone somewhere was wielding pens and brushes to produce all of this fun and entertainment, this humor, this action and adventure. And that mysterious somebody became my fantasy the way other kids dreamed about being big-league baseball players.

This was a time long before videos and Nintendo, so drawing was foremost among my innocent boyhood diversions. My friend Randy and I spent long afternoons entertaining ourselves with nothing but pencil and paper. I'd draw a scene, a room in detail, say, then fold the sheet over and draw the identical scene with dramatic changes — a monster appears at the window, the dog keels over dead, the flower grows a hand. These mini-movies were silly, but they cracked us up. Randy and I would exchange our drawings and then roll on the floor in stitches.

I was a troublemaker in school. My grades were A's and B's, except in conduct. I chewed gum in class. I passed notes. Naturally my artistic talent played a part in my mischief. The photographs of Khrushchev, Eisenhower, and Adlai Stevenson in *My Weekly Reader* became cross-eyed mutants or demented and deranged zombies with blackened teeth and exquisitely rendered pupils with highlights in the irises. Even in art classes I could never be serious. In my version of the standard still life of a wine bottle surrounded by fruit, the apple always said something to the banana. Sometimes our junior high art instructor drafted students to pose for figure drawing. One of the models, a particularly overweight girl, stretched out in her tights. I drew her carefully but made her even chubbier and added a pug snout, a curly tail, and an apple in her mouth.

Angrily my art teacher demanded, "Mr. Marlette, what do you want to be when you grow up?"

"An artist," I answered.

"You'll never make it," she scoffed. "You don't have the discipline!"

That was the day I decided to become a professional artist. "You can'ts" and "you'll nevers" from teachers and parents have squelched and discouraged a lot of people, but they have also galvanized more young talent than any encouragement ever could.

My high school years were spent drawing the Beatles, the Dave Clark Five, the Animals, and the Rolling Stones. The day after the Beatles appeared for the first time on "The Ed Sullivan Show" in 1964, every cow-eyed adolescent girl in my algebra class gave me fifty cents a pop to draw Paul McCartney. I had graduated from desserts and marbles. It was a great way to impress the girls, show my devotion to rock and roll without actually having to dance in front of people, and pick up extra spending money.

And if rock and roll was the hymn of my adolescence, *Mad* magazine became my Bible. Its satire of TV, Madison Avenue, Hollywood, and cigarette manufacturers was just irreverent enough to be an antidote to the powerlessness of puberty. *Mad* legitimized skepticism toward authority and probably sowed the cynicism that flowered fully in the Woodstock generation. Mort Drucker's great caricatures and the wild, juicy comic drawings of Jack Davis and Wally Wood were my models. I practiced the *Mad* style by drawing caricatures of TV celebrities and politicians. I wrote and illustrated a parody of "The Man from U.N.C.L.E." and concocted a comic book parody of the "Batman" TV series, called "Ratman," which featured a notorious dandruff-specked geek at school and several of my teachers. My friends laughed at "Ratman," but one of them said scornfully, "You spent your weekend doing this?"

I was a miserable failure as a teenager. I wasn't captain of the football team. I didn't date a cheerleader. I couldn't even get my face to break out. I was five years behind everyone else going through puberty. When all the guys in my high school gym class were growing hair on their chest and cruising the Dairy Queen to pick up chicks, I still thought the Dairy Queen was for ice cream. My voice didn't change until I was in my thirties. On the phone people mistook me for Minnie Mouse on helium.

I suspect all satirists were lousy teenagers. I've never met one without the scars of a high school geek or nerd. Ours is the rage flowing from narcissistic injury. Pride is our wound and revenge our motive. I survived my own adolescence because I knew somehow that this — high school misery — was not it. High school was not the final word on me. So I threw myself into learning my future trade.

Cartooning can't be taught. You learn by studying the work of the masters and trying to emulate them. In high school I started collecting cartoons, "swipes" as we call them in the trade. Not to be confused with plagiarism, which is scorned, swiping is more what Igor did for Dr. Frankenstein — grave-robbing body parts so you can create your own creature. With a well-stocked swipe file, even a beginner can bluff his way through a drawing by lifting a Mauldin tank here or an Oliphant jet there, piecing it together with a Jack Davis donkey or a Mort Drucker hand. ("How do you draw an undertaker? Hmm . . . didn't Ronald Searle draw one once? . . . I know it's here somewhere.")

Of course, swiping shouldn't be carried too far for too long. Some cartoonists become addicts, swipe junkies who never develop their own style. My collection of cartoon clips served primarily as inspiration. I grazed through them endlessly for the sheer joy of it, studying every detail — how Conrad drew shoes, how Oliphant drew hands, how Don Wright drew eyes, what shading techniques they used — trying to absorb by osmosis the secret magic of their work.

In high school I began talking more openly about pursuing art as a career. Naturally, my mother and father were alarmed. They were Depression-era parents who believed in working for a living, and drawing did not seem like work to them. Actually it didn't seem like work to me either — thus the appeal.

I sold my first cartoon, which featured the high school swim coaches, to the local newspaper for four dollars and was soon earning money from my drawings on a regular basis. As I became less of a financial burden to my parents, they relaxed a bit. To their credit, they always insisted I do what I want to do for a living.

But I faced another obstacle: the ritual interrogation by the high school guidance counselor, during which we students had to lay out our hopes, dreams, and aspirations so he could squash them like bugs. He browsed through my permanent record and said, "And what do you want to do when you graduate, Mr. Marlette?"

"Go to college."

"And what do you want to be when you finish college?"

"A cartoonist," I chirped.

"I see," he said, barely disguising his disappointment.

He put down my file folder, crossed his arms, and leaned forward in his chair. "Douglas, I realize you have some talent in that area," he began, "but I feel I must warn you — when you go off to college, you'll find that artists are a dime a dozen." He paused to allow this to sink in. "Now, your test scores indicate some math ability. Why don't you go into architecture? It would utilize your drafting and math skills. And if you still want to pursue this . . . this cartooning as a hobby, you can do it at home at nights or on weekends."

"Yessir." I smiled, thanked him, and never gave his advice a second thought. Didn't he know we cartoonists never listen to authority figures?

I enrolled at Seminole Community College so I could work part-time in the art department of the *Orlando Sentinel.* As low man on the totem pole I meticulously cut color overlays, pasted up weather maps, air-brushed into oblivion buttocks and excess cleavage in movie ads, or removed obscene gestures and horse testicles from photos to make them suitable for a family newspaper. But it wasn't all drudgery. I also drew cartoon illustrations known as "dingbats" to decorate the editorial page and news stories. Performing regularly on deadline helped sharpen my cartoon thinking skills, if not my grade point average.

When I transferred to Florida State University I sought out the student newspaper, the *Flambeau,* and immediately began doing editorial cartoons on everything from the war in Indochina to local police brutality to coed dormitories on campus. Like many students of that era, I was trying to make sense of the times and the values I had inherited against the backdrop of a senseless war and corruption and duplicity in high places. I never actually joined Students for a Democratic Society — I was too much of an anarchist to join a

"ONLY ONE THING CAN GET THESE HANDS CLEAN..."

RED WHITE & BLUE

SILENT MAJORITY

SOFTSOAP

YOU CAN COUNT ON IT TO REMAIN SILENT!

VIETNAM ATROCITIES

"PICKY, PICKY, PICKY!!"

10,000 AMERICANS DEAD IN VIETNAM —UNDER NIXON ADMINISTRATION

VIETNAM MORATORIUM

"AM AH MISTAKEN OR DID THAT CHILD SAY, 'UP AGAINST THE WALL, WHITEY?'"

MISSISSIPPI

"IT'S A GIRL!"

club — but with Nixon in the White House, and the *Love It or Leave It* bumper sticker mentality of Vice President Spiro Agnew and his Silent Majority loose in the land, it was impossible not to take sides. When Nixon, elected on a peace platform, escalated the war in Indochina, even southern campuses like FSU, which traditionally could be counted on to support whatever war a president was waging, erupted in protest.

On November 15, 1969, I hitched a ride in a Volkswagen bus painted camouflage green and loaded with wine, weed, and strangers and drove all night to Washington, D.C., for the Vietnam Moratorium March Against Death. At the foot of the Washington Monument half a million of us "kids," as the media called us, gathered to protest the war, singing, "All we are saying is give peace a chance."

"Are you listenin', Mr. Nixon?" Pete Seeger called out between refrains of the John Lennon lyric.

He wasn't. But the trip wasn't a total wash. Between marching by candlelight to Arlington Cemetery and catching my first whiff of tear gas at Dupont Circle, I visited another Washington monument — Herblock. Herbert L. Block had been nailing Nixon in the *Washington Post* since before our parents bought their first copy of Dr. Spock. When I entered Herblock's cluttered office and saw his sketches for the next day's cartoon about Nixon's reaction to our peace march, I thought I'd scaled Parnassus and glimpsed Zeus in action. Herb signed a copy of that day's drawing, looked at my cartoons, and told me I had a good line and to keep plugging. All the way back to Tallahassee, I had a Herblock contact high. Maybe we hadn't stopped the war, but I had met perhaps the greatest cartoonist of this century.

Drawing on deadline several times a week for the *Flambeau* forced me to produce. And the only way to learn to draw cartoons is to draw cartoons. Just as a writer must discover his or her "voice," so must a cartoonist. And under the pressure of that regimen I felt the first stirrings of mine. I remember when I heard it for the first time, when idea, image, drawing, and delivery all came together.

The new Disney World theme park was opening in central Florida, and news reports were speculating about the impact it would have on the surrounding area. The headlines were also filled with the poverty and degradation of the state's

"HEY, FELLA! WHICH WAY TO THE MAGIC KINGDOM?"

migrant worker population. I drew a touristy-looking Mickey Mouse greeting a family of poor black migrants sitting on the porch of their ramshackle digs. "Hey, Fella! Which way to the Magic Kingdom?" Mickey asks. That was me. That was Marlette. Such moments were few and far between, but that was one of them.

Soon the College Press Service, a student press syndicate service, began distributing my cartoons to college newspapers around the country and to underground publications like Boston's *Phoenix, The Great Speckled Bird* in Atlanta, and the *LA Free Press*.

I was majoring in art, and my roommates were particularly fascinated by the figure drawing classes I was taking. They had heard about the live nude models and wanted details.

"What was it like?" they asked when I returned from my first studio session. "Are the models really buck nekkid?"

"Uh-huh," I assured them, "they're nude all right."

They were intrigued. But the more curious they grew, the more I played down the eroticism of naked women models, insisting that the nudity quickly became routine and not at all titillating.

"It's all very boring really," I said, "like working on logarithms or balancing a checkbook."

One day all three of my roommates were studying at their desks. They watched me gather up my art supplies, and as I was leaving with my sketch pad under my arm, one of them said, "Where you going — figure drawing class?"

"Uh-huh."

"Good-looking models?" He leered.

"Yep!"

"You sound excited!" he probed.

"I am," I said. "This is a very special day."

"Why?"

"Because," I said as I closed the door, "today we practice tracing."

The more convinced I became that I could work as a political cartoonist, the less my art courses seemed to matter. When the fine arts program turned me down flat because my portfolio was contaminated with too many cartoons, I changed my major to philosophy. Socrates became my hero, and "The unexamined life is not worth living" my motto. Reading political philosophers like Plato, Aristotle, Locke, Hobbes,

I CHANGED MY MAJOR TO PHILOSOPHY

and Rousseau seemed more relevant than drawing naked ladies.

In those turbulent times it was hard not to be political, especially when your number in the draft lottery was ten. And my politics definitely found their way into my cartoons in the *Flambeau*. The ancient Chinese curse, "May you live in interesting times" is no curse for political cartoonists. What was lousy for the nation was wonderful for a hungry young cartoonist. I cut my drawing teeth on the lies of Lyndon Johnson and Richard Nixon and this nation's war with Vietnam and with itself. Our best leaders were assassinated, and our worst got elected. There was wickedness in high places, murder and mayhem abroad, polarization and despair in the land. The issues were life and death then, or seemed to be, and the choices between right and wrong clear-cut.

I may not have known a lot back then, but as graduation approached I did know one thing. I was no Benjamin Braddock in *The Graduate* — confused about career choices and the course my life should take. I knew exactly what I wanted to do. I wanted to become a political cartoonist, and I was ready to take on the world.

Only one thing stood in my way: the military draft. My father was a Marine Corps lifer, so my views on the war in Vietnam created a lot of tension in my family. But one thing was certain in my mind: the war was wrong and I wasn't going. When I went before my local draft board to register as a conscientious objector, they found it hard to believe I had picked up subversive notions like Love Thine Enemy and Thou Shalt Not Kill at the First Baptist Church Sunday school. Unlike the Quakers, we Southern Baptists aren't exactly known for our long-standing pacifist tradition. Pass the Lord and Praise the Ammunition was more our style. I had to give evidence of the "sincerity" of my beliefs, including any public statement or record of such beliefs. Along with letters and testimony from family, friends, teachers, and ministers, I submitted my political cartoons.

As I sat across from the draft board, a dour lot, headed by Florida's only female commandant in the American Legion, baring my nineteen-year-old soul, letting my drawings do most of the talking, I could tell they were not amused. But they were convinced of my "sincerity," and they granted me

CO status — a first in my family, my church, my town, my zip code, and (it felt like) my planet. I didn't know I was getting my first and most important lesson in the codes of free expression: if you are going to take a stand on controversial public matters, drawing pictures that take Judeo-Christian values seriously and speaking out in a direct, unvarnished way, buddy, you better get used to tough audiences.

MY DRAFT BOARD WAS NOT AMUSED

YEARBOOK

When I was at Florida State University, we "liberated" our traditional college annual, the *Tally Ho*, from its slavishly stuffy class pictures and its emphasis on sports and fraternity and sorority pictures (after all, they promoted a class society, and we believed a university was supposed to be egalitarian and classless). Our long-haired, tie-dyed, love-beaded staff chose a more democratic (and lower-priced) paperback cover, turning our yearbook into a pamphlet for our own counter-culture agendas. I hear that this annual, with my illustration on its cover, is now a collector's item among devotees.

Talkin' 'bout my g-g-g-generation!

BOTH GUNS BLAZING

CARTOONING IS MORE than just drawing funny pictures. A cartoonist makes others see the world through his eyes by having a distinct point of view. I suppose I came by mine naturally. I've always had something of the rebel in me. I can relate to Marlon Brando in *The Wild One,* when he is asked, "What are you rebelling against?" "Whaddaya got?" he answers. It's probably in my genes; my grandmother was bayoneted by a National Guardsman for agitating during a mill strike.

In the South, rebellion is part of the cultural landscape, like trailer parks and barbecue joints. The South gave us many of the greatest resisters and revolutionaries: Thomas Jefferson, Patrick Henry, Francis Marion, Robert E. Lee, Stonewall Jackson, and Martin Luther King, Jr. Not only did the South secede from the Union, but one county I lived in actually seceded from the Confederacy as well, waging war on Yankees, Confederates, and everybody else.

As a teenager growing up on the red clay battlefields of the civil rights movement, I was haunted by the ghosts of the great southern insurrections of the past. My people, the family who raised me and taught me

THE GHOSTS OF THE GREAT SOUTHERN INSURRECTIONS OF THE PAST HAUNTED MY TEENAGE YEARS...

right from wrong, were on the wrong side of that great debate. The volatility of that time was played out not just on the nightly newscasts and daily headlines but also at my supper table and in the lives of people I knew. Jones County, Mississippi, where I once lived, was headquarters for the militant White Knights of the Ku Klux Klan. Friends of my family were suspected of being Klan members and had their phones tapped by the FBI. I remember a gym class when one of my classmates left school red-faced and tearstained because the FBI had arrested his father in connection with the murders of civil rights workers Goodman, Schwerner, and Chaney.

My grandfather, at various times a cotton farmer, mill worker, surveyor, and deputy sheriff, was also a yellow-dog Democrat and New Dealer who had voted for Franklin D. Roosevelt four times, ". . . and if he was runnin' today I'd vote for him again!"

"Why is that, Granddaddy?"

"'Cause he was the only president we ever had who cared anything about the poor man." As my eyes misted up with populist sentimentality, he added, "'Course, his only mistake was he shoulda' let Hitler kill them Jews!"

My grandfather was part of that long-standing southern populist tradition of identifying and sympathizing with the common man — as long as he is white and Christian. Perhaps the contradictions and ironies so vivid in the culture I was raised in brought out in me the satirist's rage and an impulse to "picture" those inconsistencies. I was forced early to think about what I believed, and going against the grain in those small towns of the Deep South cost you something. Political opinions were more than just armchair posturing or cocktail party pontification; they affected my life and the life of my community.

Had I grown up in a different time, in a different place, I might have ended up drawing a comic strip about cats. But for me drawing funny pictures was not enough; I hoped I could use my drawings to understand life, not just to be distracted from it. I wanted my cartoons to challenge people, to make them think as well as laugh.

When I was starting out, not only were the times a-changing but American political cartooning was undergoing a fundamental change as well. When an Australian named Pat

GOING AGAINST THE GRAIN IN THOSE SMALL TOWNS OF THE DEEP SOUTH COST YOU SOMETHING

Oliphant came to America and joined the *Denver Post* in 1964, he touched off a revolution. He drew in a contemporary British/Australian style, with a dash of *Mad* magazine's Jack Davis thrown in. Unlike the cartoons we were used to, with their heavy messages — Uncle Sam rolling up his sleeves, trudging into swamps labeled "the economy" or "Vietnam," whatever; clouds labeled "cloud," trees labeled "tree," labels labeled "label" — Oliphant's draftsmanship, caricature, and bite were distinctive. I was hooked. Oliphant captured the irreverence of the times and reflected the sensibility of the new TV generation. The cartoonists like me who were coming of age seized on the Oliphant attitude and ran with it.

Of course, Oliphant was simply part of the great tradition of political cartoonists — renegades, mavericks, challengers — who defied the powers that be and questioned authority. Back in the nineteenth century Honoré Daumier was thrown into the slammer for his scandalous drawings of King Louis-Philippe. An emissary of the corrupt politician Boss Tweed offered Thomas Nast half a million dollars to study art in Europe. Nast had almost singlehandedly driven Tweed from office. "Most of my constituents can't read," Tweed said, "but them damned pictures!" In the twentieth century Art Young was tried for sedition by the Wilson administration for his antiwar cartoons in *The Masses*; Hitler put a price on the head of British cartoonist David Low; and Richard Nixon planned his election campaign around erasing the image Herblock had created of him. These artists' simple drawings said so much with so little, and they packed quite a wallop.

After finishing college I was free to pursue my cartooning career. I got a job drawing maps and charts and occasional political cartoons for the *St. Petersburg Times,* hoping that someday they would create a full-time editorial cartooning slot for me. In the whole country there are only about two hundred or so positions for cartoonists, and maybe only ten at newspapers where I would feel at home editorially. Cartoonists tend to draw for one newspaper until they drop or retire, so when a spot opens up, a swarm of dissatisfied veterans and lean and hungry wannabees descend. Competition is fierce, and finding a job often has as much to do with timing and luck as with talent.

A job did open up soon, but not in St. Petersburg; it was at the *Charlotte Observer* in North Carolina. All I knew about the *Observer* was that it was the Carolinas' largest paper, was part of the Knight newspaper chain (now Knight-Ridder), and was known as a moderate southern paper. Under C. A. (Pete) McKnight's leadership the *Observer* had taken some unpopular stands on school desegregation and had supported progressive political leadership when such views were costly. I sent off a batch of cartoons, and right after my twenty-second birthday, just six months out of college, I began working there.

Within a year, my antiwar, pro-amnesty, anti-death penalty cartoons had created such a stir that John S. Knight, owner of the newspaper chain, and his brother, absentee *Observer* publisher James L. Knight, wanted me fired. News stories or editorials that run against the grain are one thing, but challenging the status quo in pictures is quite another.

"Some twenty-two-year-old kid comes into town with both guns blazing," John Knight grumbled from his corporate aerie in Miami. His brother Jim, a notorious reactionary famous for his lack of sympathy toward those who did not share his skin color, was more direct. "Why you keep that guy I'll never know," he taunted an *Observer* manager in a letter. "I think you guys are afraid of him."

Actually they were in a bind. My cartoons were already being picked up occasionally by *Time* and *Newsweek,* the *Washington Post* and the *New York Times,* bringing the paper a national profile it had not previously enjoyed. The *Observer* also wanted to maintain its moderately progressive reputation — as rare as sushi franchises in the South then — to attract talented young journalists fresh out of college who would work cheaply. My cartoons had become something of a symbol of the *Observer*'s commitment to free speech and its tolerance of unpopular ideas. Reneging on that would seriously damage that image.

My editors defended me to the Knights, arguing that my

Bombs Away

FIRST CHARLOTTE OBSERVER CARTOON

NORTH CAROLINA WAS THE FIRST STATE IN RECENT HISTORY TO EXECUTE A WOMAN (A MOTHER)

cartoons were popular with the younger readers the *Observer* wanted to attract. They didn't cave in to the owners' pressure, but they moved my cartoons from the editorial page to the op-ed page, "putting distance between Marlette and the masthead," they explained privately, while telling readers the move gave them more flexibility with layout. The op-ed page, Jules Feiffer points out, "has developed into a ghetto in which newspapers confine strong opinion. This is a free press way of apologizing to its readers for the First Amendment."

After a couple of years I realized the dream of every young cartoonist — syndication! King Features Syndicate, the largest and oldest syndicate in the country, would sell and distribute my cartoons to other newspapers. Syndicates usually collect the revenues and, believe it or not, split them fifty-fifty with the cartoonist. The larger the newspaper, the more they pay for a feature. For instance, the *Boston Globe* may pay seventy dollars a week for a cartoonist's work while the Moss Point, Mississippi, paper gets the same cartoons for five dollars a week. The number of papers that buy the cartoon is significant, but the sizes of the papers on the list may be more important. One hundred newspapers with good-sized circulations may be a better, more lucrative list than two hundred tiny papers.

Someone in the newsroom once asked a reporter if I was really involved with a syndicate. She shuddered, thinking about hit men and horse heads under bedsheets. "But he seems like such a nice guy!" she said. This same person was stunned when she learned that Paul McCartney was in a band before Wings.

I arrived in Charlotte just after the landmark busing decision *Swann* v. *Board of Education,* when the community was divided and local cartoon material was plentiful. And for the next eight years I drew on everything from busing to brown lung, from PTL to Jesse Helms, from local and state idiocies to the presidencies of Nixon, Ford, Carter, and Reagan. With those kinds of subjects to call on, I almost couldn't help establishing a lot of freedom for myself editorially.

Still, I was getting a little restless, so I applied for a Nieman Fellowship at Harvard. Nieman Fellows spend an entire academic year with the treasures of Harvard at their disposal. They have faculty status, which gives them the run of the campus and allows them to dip into any course at the

NIEMAN REPORTS

VOL. XLIII, NO. 1 SPRING 1989

university. The cliché about the midcareer Nieman sabbatical is that it is the best year of your life. I signed up for Anthony Lewis's First Amendment law course at Harvard Law School, and for courses on moral and social inquiry in the Core Curriculum and American populism at the Kennedy School of Government, both taught by the splendid and renowned child psychiatrist Robert Coles. I sat in on theologian Harvey Cox's course in liberation theology at the Divinity School. Three times a week the Nieman program invites scholars, journalists, authors, artists, and politicians to Walter Lippmann House for intimate lunches, dinners, and wine and cheese seminars. We schmoozed with Hodding Carter and Pat Derian, Jules Feiffer, Art Buchwald, Seymour Hersh, Oriana Fallaci, John Kenneth Galbraith, Julia Child, Vincente Minnelli, Alan Pakula, John Updike, and John Irving. I'll never forget the night I sat next to Robert Penn Warren at dinner and later held the lamp so he could read his poetry, or the time B.B. King performed an impromptu blues concert in the upstairs library. Added to this was the time I spent with the other Nieman Fellows, top American journalists as well as a handful of Niemans from other countries.

By the end of my sabbatical I was refreshed and stimulated but ready to return to Charlotte. I was getting homesick for Jim and Tammy Bakker. Their burgeoning ministry was entering its Golden Age — they had just installed gold bathroom fixtures in their new Palm Beach condo — and I wanted to be there to chronicle it. I got back in time to catch the purchases of the houseboat, the Mercedes, and the Rolls Royce as well as the grand opening of the religious theme park they built outside Charlotte (Six Flags over Jesus, someone called it) and the christening of the water slide.

I was back in the editorial cartooning saddle, lampooning PTL and others, and I also launched my comic strip, "Kudzu," named for the vine that covers the South. I spent the next few years adjusting to the deadline demands of two full-time jobs.

After fifteen years in Charlotte, just when I was growing a little restless again, I got a phone call that changed my life. It was from Bill Kovach, who had just been named editor of the Atlanta *Journal-Constitution*. His appointment had led people to believe that owner Anne Cox Chambers, who had been Jimmy Carter's ambassador to Belgium and was one of the world's richest women, was sick and tired of apologizing to the Grahams and Sulzbergers of the journalistic world for the pissant quality of her Atlanta flagship. Bringing in Kovach was a way of winning instant respectability.

The Atlanta newspapers had always ridden on the reputation of Ralph McGill, who spoke out so eloquently against bigotry and race prejudice during the sixties. But as one observer put it, "The Atlanta papers aren't what they used to be under Ralph McGill . . . and never were!" Even when McGill was editor, the papers were so bad they actually refused to send a reporter to cover the Selma march. The masthead boast of Covering Dixie Like the Dew was a joke. For years the Atlanta papers had flacked for the hustle and hype of the city's shallow country club values and as a result had run off some of America's finest journalists, from Jack Nelson to Eugene Patterson. The papers slavishly reflected the image Atlanta had of itself as the City Too Busy to Hate, while making sure it remained the City Too Busy to Think.

One of Kovach's first moves was hiring me away from Charlotte. He was an artist himself, so he understood how strong an impact a cartoonist could have on readers; he also knew that bringing in a cartoonist known for his, shall we say, controversial views would set the swashbuckling tone the paper needed. Kovach had a great vision for making the *Journal-Constitution* into a national newspaper of the caliber of the *Washington Post, Boston Globe, New York Times,* or *Chicago Tribune.* It was music to my ears. Still, I had to ask him if he knew what kinds of hassles he was opening himself up to in working with a cartoonist.

"What do you mean?" he responded.

"You're thinking, 'Won't it be fun having kick-ass cartoons,' and you're right — it is fun. But what happens when you're woken up on a Sunday morning with reader complaints? Or worse, advertiser complaints. What about dealing with pressures from advertiser-sensitive publishers? What about not being able to go to dinner at the City Club without hearing, 'Why don't you fire Marlette?' What about getting letters and phone calls and visits from community leaders and politicians because of a goddamn cartoon?"

Bill listened, reached over and picked up my cartoons

from his desk, and flipped through them again. After a moment he looked up and said, "I can handle it." And he did. Cartoonists pray for editors like Bill Kovach.

In transforming the *Journal-Constitution* Kovach had his work cut out for him. Those of us who shared his dream for the papers were brimming with hope and energy. Word spread quickly, and applications to join the Kovach enterprise came pouring in by the thousands. At the same time the local Good Ol' Boy network circled the wagons. Kovach ruffled the feathers of these Bubbas by committing the cardinal southern sin of aspiring to greatness. They thought he was putting on airs, acting uppity and, worse, suggesting that they were something short of magnificent.

When he got rid of a few of the paper's many columnists, most of them card-carrying Bubbas (some of us said Kovach had committed "Bubbacide"), to make room for more news, the network closed ranks. Echoing the old-time segregationists' whine, they called the Kovach team "outsiders" and "New Yorkers coming down here to tell us how to run our newspapers." Never mind that all of us so-called outsiders and New Yorkers were from places like Alabama, Tennessee, and North Carolina. Stars-and-Bars-waving patriotism is the last refuge of the southern bigot.

Even so, it was a heady time for us in Atlanta. Under Kovach's leadership we were Pulitzer finalists that first year in a record five categories, and I brought the paper its first Pulitzer Prize in twenty years. The following year the paper won a second Pulitzer for a stunning investigation of dis-

"YOU NEED TO SPEAK TO ONE OF OUR LOAN OFFICERS!"

criminatory loan practices by Atlanta banks, which sent a
clear message to the local power structure that the paper had
resigned from the unofficial country club it had long be-
longed to.

When the 1988 Democratic National Convention was held in Atlanta, we covered it
like no one had covered conventions before.
After months of planning and organization,
Kovach had us ready. The journalism world
had voiced great skepticism about the Atlanta
newspapers experiment, but we blew them
away. Walter Cronkite told Anne Cox
Chambers that he had never seen as fine a job
of coverage as ours. The South finally had the
kind of newspaper it deserved, and it was
being accomplished by southerners.

In Atlanta I got to ride herd on some new
sacred cattle. The *Charlotte Observer* worried about offend-
ing the banks and Duke Power Company, but the *Journal-
Constitution* fretted over the feelings of Coca-Cola, University
of Georgia football, Delta Airlines, Georgia Power, and the
black political establishment.

" IT'S BEEN ONE OF THOSE WEEKS!"

My free-wheeling cattle prod was particularly tough for
the editorial page editor to take. A Cox holdover, he was
panic-stricken about losing control. If it weren't for the fact
that I had been hired directly by Kovach, he would have
made endless trouble for me. Instead he was merely a nui-
sance. But without Kovach keeping him at bay, some of the

best cartoons I drew in Atlanta would never have seen the light of print.

At one moment, however, he was very helpful. I used him to figure out what to include and what to leave out in my Pulitzer entry. His judgments were unerring: everything he said not to submit I entered; everything he said to enter I left out. And sure enough I won.

The Kovach years in Atlanta were great, but, not surprisingly, they had to end. We were upsetting too many powerful people. Kovach wasn't turning out to be the lapdog the Cox owners thought they had hired; before long they found they had a Great Dane on their hands, and he was out of control. When they realized that Kovach was not their kind of team player, they started pulling the plug. Firing Kovach would make them look bad, so they set him up by pushing their vision of a *USA Today*–type McNewspaper, reneging on the five-year plan they had used to entice him to Atlanta, making drastic cuts in budgets and the news hole, and second-guessing him relentlessly. Finally Kovach resigned.

That day was the saddest of my career, and a tragedy for journalism and the South. Our Camelot was over. But it didn't go out with a whimper. Staff members signed petitions protesting the owners' policy and paid for full-page ads to publicize their grievances. A march and rally (which made the national TV news) brought hundreds of Atlantans downtown to support the ousted editor, an unprecedented event in the history of American journalism.

Bill Kovach is now curator of the Nieman Foundation at Harvard, and the Atlanta papers are headed by a former editor of *USA Today*. Warner Brothers is making a movie about the Kovach story. Pat Conroy and Pulitzer Prize–winning reporter Wendell Rawls wrote the screenplay, and Robert Redford has signed on to play Kovach.

With Kovach out, I knew I had to move on, as did many others in the next months. Management let me know none too subtly that there was a price for having spoken out at the rally.

After being burned by Atlanta, I found myself headed for the town that erects statues to, names schools after, and otherwise honors and reveres General William T. Sherman — the Big Apple. *Newsday*, the excellent Long Island newspaper, was moving into Manhattan in a big way with its New York edition and was looking for a cartoonist to join battle.

When I told my friends and family I was moving North, they were stunned. Then I said North meant New York City, and they were horrified. I might as well have been getting a sex change operation. Nobody gasped audibly and reeled back in horror, but I could see it in their eyes. "You'll be mugged!" "You'll be homeless!" "You'll live in a cardboard box!" "You'll become a crack dealer!" As a rule, southerners are suspicious of life in the big city. In fact, we are the best haters of New York City in the world, except perhaps for New Yorkers.

I have never met a southerner who didn't have an I-Loathe-New-York story. Our worst nightmares about the city always seem to come true during our first visit. When southerners come to town we get mugged at the La Guardia baggage claim. Son of Sam is driving the cab we hail. By the time we check into our hotel, the Reverend Al Sharpton is suing us. One North Carolina friend arrived just in time to see a wrecking ball knock down the hotel he was booked into. Another friend visiting from Georgia heard a woman screaming from an apartment above the street, "Help me! Help me! He's killing me! He's killing me!" Like any chivalrous son of the South, he gallantly rushed into the dark building and burst through the apartment door—into a group-therapy primal scream session. The therapist threatened to call the cops. As for me, within a few hours of arriving on Manhattan island for the first time to sign my syndication contract, I was propositioned by, yes, a bisexual male porno filmmaker. Welcome to the Big Apple.

My neighbor in Decatur, Georgia, Bruce Wilson, an attorney who has a fondness for guns, expressed it best. "I've done a lot of things in my life — some good, some not," he explained, politely declining an invitation to visit us in our new hometown. "But when I die I hope I can look back on my life and be proud to say I never set foot in New York City."

My southern roots are deep, too, and I never figured I'd spend much time north of the Mason-Dixon — certainly not in New York. But I never had quite the same revulsion for Yankees or the Big Apple that some of my kinsmen do. I was always attracted to the city's energy, excitement, and vitality. Artists are naturally drawn to New York. It's The Show, the storm center of human achievement. And it holds a special place in the dreams of my youth.

I first visited New York through TV, movies, books, and magazines. The media initiated me into its secrets, mysteries, and allure. I learned about Macy's from *Miracle on 34th Street*. I knew that Rob and Laura Petrie of "The Dick Van Dyke Show" lived in suburban New Rochelle. *Mad* magazine's offices were on Lexington Avenue, and they made fun of the admen on Madison Avenue. Holden Caulfield and the Glass children in J. D. Salinger's novels actually grew up on the streets of Manhattan. I saw the city through the comic prisms of Neil Simon and Woody Allen. Johnny Carson ribbed the Long Island Railroad and Con Ed, and those impossibly sophisticated *New Yorker* cartoons informed my sense of humor. In the sweltering southern summers of my youth, Jules Feiffer's drawings spoke to me.

The comedians on Ed Sullivan and "The Tonight Show" all seemed to share some wonderful inside joke, with their Jewish cultural references and Yiddish expressions that I knew I would be able to understand if I could only go to New York. Those places and references became as much a part of the geography of my imagination as were Judea and Samaria in my Sunday school lessons or Vicksburg and Chancellorsville in my history books. And I imbued those alien landscapes and cultures with a vitality and reality that seemed achingly absent from my own.

I sometimes compare notes and swap cracker credentials with my friend and fellow southerner, novelist Pat Conroy. He and I trade stories from our white-boy roots in that trailer park of the spirit we remember as our childhood. In the wonderful tradition artists and writers have of transforming self-pity into amusing anecdotes, we exchange stories of our up-from-slavery upbringings with almost a stunned disbelief. We're like survivors of a genealogical plane crash going over the details in our memory, checking with ourselves to make sure they really happened and that we survived.

We try to outdo each other with lurid recitals of family degradation and humiliation. Conroy weighs in with tales from his tortured youth, most of which have something to do with southern families who eat their young, as he has chronicled in his best-selling novels. I counter with stories about my grandmother, the one who was bayoneted by a National Guardsman during a mill strike. "Mama Gracie,"

as we called her, dipped snuff, packed a .38 in her purse,
tyrannized her family with tears and rages, and never let us
grandyoung'uns step inside her house without taking off our
shoes. Like Tammy Faye Bakker, she could weep at will, and
she wielded this mighty weapon like a truncheon. She was a
virtuoso of manipulation, a museum of hysterical symptoms.
She suffered psychosomatic illnesses, dreams, visions, and
premonitions. A tour guide of the emotions, she specialized
in the guilt trip and made sure all of us were frequent flyers.
We grandyoung'uns often prayed for a bayonet.

Mama Gracie had the big house, and my granddaddy, her
husband, lived in the little house fifteen feet out back. We
always visited her first and then went to see him. Granddaddy
and Mama Gracie never spoke to each other, never even
acknowledged one another, and never divorced. We
grandyoung'uns joked that they were staying together until
the children were dead. It was remarkable that these two had
produced eleven children, some of whom had died in infancy.
Others were claimed by alcohol, drugs, madness, and suicide.
When one of my uncles broke out of the mill town and went
off to college, even earning a master's degree, he immediately
contracted a rare, incurable disease and died. Success in this
family was a crime punishable by death.

For many southerners, New York is the place they flee to
in order to escape the overbearing presence of that kind of
past, the madness of families and towns that are too much
with them. They come here to lose themselves in the vast
anonymity of the city. I understand that impulse, but that's
not why I'm here. New York is an opportunity, not an
escape. After all, Thomas Nast invented editorial cartooning
right here.

Still, people often think of me as a "southern" cartoonist,
whatever that means. I have never sat down at the drawing
board to chronicle the folkways and mores of Dixie — to
catalogue humorous and colorful items from below the Mason-Dixon, like some Stuckey's souvenir shop of the funny
pages, but I am attracted to the issues of race, religion, and
family that are so prevalent in that region. How can you
grow up in the South and not be? But aren't those issues as
important to midtown Manhattan and Long Island as they
are to Peachpit, Georgia?

I have long suspected that Malcolm X was right: the South
is everywhere south of the Canadian border. The jarring

MAMA GRACIE

THE BIG APPLE

"LISTEN TO THIS POLL, HONEY— LAST YEAR ONE OUT OF TWO NEW YORKERS WERE VICTIMS OF CRIME!"

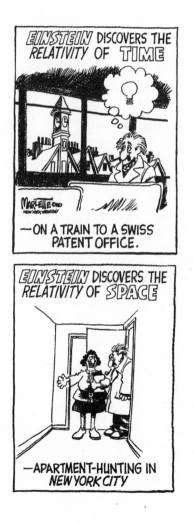

EINSTEIN DISCOVERS THE RELATIVITY OF TIME

—ON A TRAIN TO A SWISS PATENT OFFICE.

EINSTEIN DISCOVERS THE RELATIVITY OF SPACE

—APARTMENT-HUNTING IN NEW YORK CITY

"White" and "Colored" signs on the water fountains where I grew up and the poverty and ignorance that crippled the spirit of the region were just vivid symptoms of a disease that afflicts the nation as a whole. Forsyth County isn't very far from Howard Beach.

In a way, moving North gave me a feeling I'd experienced before. In the sixties the South was the nation's whipping boy. We wore our private demons and public neuroses on our sleeves, and the world had something to point at. However, over the last few years, as the South has homogenized itself into the Sunbelt, it is slowly giving up the role of America's designated punching bag.

Now New York City has claimed that position in America's unconscious. New York bashing is a national sport. For all its glitz, glamour, and opportunity, the city's problems have grown to such a magnitude — drugs, crime, homelessness, racism, greed, corruption — that New York has become what Mississippi was in the sixties: America's problem child, the scapegoat, a mess. The issues loom large. The contradictions, ironies, and hypocrisies are as vivid in New York as the ones I saw during my childhood. They stand out in stark and stunning relief.

It's all a caricature — a cartoon really. New York City is Toontown. This southerner feels right at home.

THE CULT OF THE REFRIGERATOR AND THE BATHROOM BLUES

W HEN CARTOONISTS DIE, our souls go to that great refrigerator door in the sky. The highest compliment that you can pay us is to hang our work on the refrigerator door. Never mind how many newspapers syndicate us. Never mind the Pulitzers we've won, honorary degrees we've received, or lunch boxes, tote bags, greeting cards, and plush toys we've appeared on. A cartoonist's success is measured by the number of refrigerators he decorates.

Actually, we cartoonists are a simple folk with simple needs, other than our desire for universal praise and admiration. We are pleased if a drawing makes our readers smile. And if they double over clutching their stomachs, gasping for air, and making funny snorting sounds through their nose, we are ecstatic. But if they cut out the cartoon and hang it on the refrigerator with little plastic magnets shaped like fruit, we achieve cartoonists' nirvana. On refrigerator doors around the country, alongside Mom's special recipes and Junior's fingerpainting, hang yellowed clippings of cherished comic strips, beloved *New Yorker* panels, and favorite political cartoons assaulting the owner's least favorite public figures. Low-calorie Lean Cuisines and low-fat yogurt may be stored inside, but out front is a feast for the funnybone, a smorgasbord for the soul. Refrigerators are our Nielsen ratings.

Nobody else except Weight Watchers gives the common refrigerator as much significance as cartoonists do. They can even play a pivotal role

---

in a simple evening out. When someone invites us to their home for the first time, we make a beeline for the kitchen. Skip the introductions and forget the pleasantries. We can find the Frigidaire faster than Roseanne Barr. Our hosts, unaccustomed to cartoonists in their home, may innocently assume that we are hungry and offer us hors d'oeuvres as we knock over furniture in our desperate search for the fridge. But it is not food we are after. Amana and Westinghouse are our Louvre and our Metropolitan Museum. If our work is hanging there we can relax; the home we have entered is warm and friendly. We have connected with our readers. We are beloved by strangers. Of course, if a competitor's work is there, we are hurt, insulted, betrayed. We take it personally. I have seen cartoonists who failed to "make the fridge" plummet into depressions that would make Sylvia Plath look like Pollyanna. Personally, I refuse to be intimidated by a kitchen appliance. Long ago I learned to carry my own plastic strawberry and banana magnets wherever I go. I sneak them into people's homes, hang around the fridge until nobody's looking, then hang my own cartoons, removing the work of others if necessary. It's not something I am particularly proud of, but I am able to face the refrigerator and have found peace of mind.

Oddly, the only other place you can find us in the American home is the bathroom. Occasionally original cartoon drawings are hung on the wall there, and often books of cartoons are stacked by the toilet for leisurely perusal.

"I just got your book and I love it!" a lady once gushed when we first met.

"Well, thank you," I said.

"I keep it by the toilet in the bathroom!"

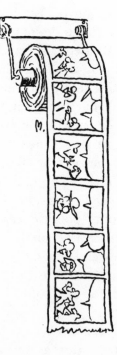

For some reason, people go out of their way to tell cartoonists that we've been consigned to the john, but we've come to regard this as a compliment. We are always being told a two-edged truth: we are loved and despised. Our work is the first thing people read in the morning, but they also think it's fit for a latrine.

To cartoonists the toilet just isn't the same as the refrigerator, which is a standing ovation. The bathroom is more complicated — more like a sitting ovation. For some reason cartoons cluster like cave paintings in the kitchen, where people ingest, and in the bathroom, where we eliminate and relieve.

Cartoons provide sustenance and relief. Do people hang drawings on refrigerators because they see them as spiritual nourishment? Do people enjoy taking in their insights? Do those who put them in the bathroom have more "anal" personalities and associate cartoons with "dumping on politicians" or "letting go?" Or are they expressing their delight and pride in the drawings, like a two-year-old with his bowel movement? Who knows? But a clue to the cartoon's archaic appeal and power is bound up in these odd rituals of putting them in the kitchen and the bathroom.

Cartoons are little windows onto the dark recesses of our souls, reminding us how human we really are. For that reason, no one ever hangs them in living rooms, not even cartoonists. People are more formal there, they're inhibited and restrained. Living rooms are for coffee table books no one reads and for pointless, decorative prints. So we celebrate the alpha and the omega of our gastrointestinal systems with these funny pictures.

Meanwhile I'm staying out of strange restrooms until somebody invents plastic fruit magnets that stick to porcelain.

HAIL TO
THE CHIEFS

CARTOONISTS ARE TO PRESIDENTS what the little boy in the Hans Christian Andersen fairy tale was to the emperor: we point out when they have no clothes. It's a dirty job, but somebody has to do it.

Our tolerance as a nation for venality seemed to peak with Richard Nixon. Presidents since Nixon have seemed to grow personally more — dare I say it? — likable. That doesn't do them a lot of good in my cartoons, though; likable translates into goofy. Jerry Ford was Ozzie Nelson (uh . . . uh . . . uh . . . Betty? . . . uh . . . where's my . . . uh . . . sweater?). He was just what we needed after Tricky Dick—a Boy Scout, the kind of guy you could invite over to grill burgers and pop a few brews. Pious Sunday school teacher Jimmy Carter was too much of a Good Boy to be a Good Ol' Boy in the classic sense (that role went to First Brother Billy), but I liked him. After all, there's something appealing about a grown man named James Earl who still goes by Jimmy. And even though Ronald (What's your sign?) Reagan was President and Leader of the Free World, you basically had to commend him for not wanting to get involved. He must have known he had no business in the White House, but he was just too darned polite to disappoint all those people who voted for him. Finally, I'm devoted to George Bush for giving us Dan Quayle. I don't care about Quayle's military service record; when this country needed somebody to make George Bush look presidential, Dan Quayle was there.

Jerry, Jimmy, Ronnie, Poppy . . . it sounds like the backfield on a Midget League football team. They say Billy Graham never met a president he didn't like. I know how he feels. From I Am Not a Crook to I Am Not a Wimp, here is a look at our presidents in my personal handmade valentines.

"I CHOSE YOU FOR MY SECRETARY OF STATE, ED, BECAUSE I THINK THAT YOU CAN BEST REPRESENT MY FOREIGN POLICY...."

1980   1990

"HEY, **WIMP**!....WHATCHA GOT IN THE LUNCH PAIL?"

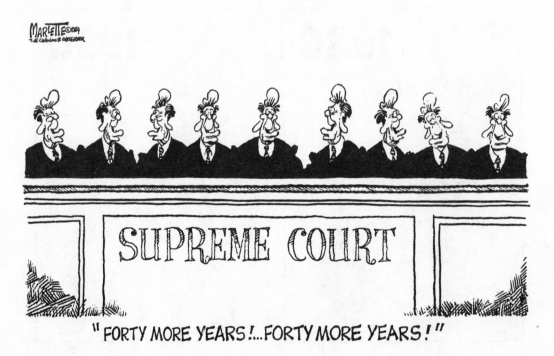

"FORTY MORE YEARS!...FORTY MORE YEARS!"

"SORRY—I'VE DEPROGRAMMED MOONIES AND I'VE DEPROGRAMMED HARE KRISHNAS, BUT THERE'S NOTHING I CAN DO WITH 'YOUTH FOR REAGAN'!"

"QUICK—GIMME A HUNDRED TWENTY BILLION QUARTERS!"

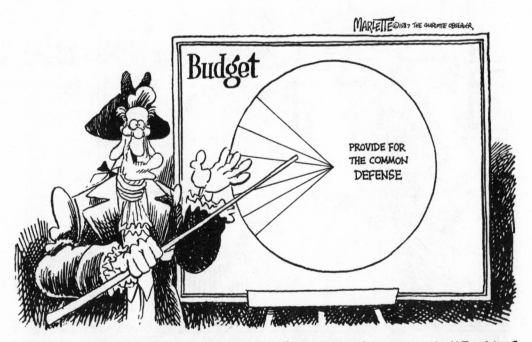

"...SO WE HAD TO CUT BACK ON FORMING A MORE PERFECT UNION, ESTABLISHING JUSTICE, PROMOTING THE GENERAL WELFARE, INSURING DOMESTIC TRANQUILITY, AND SECURING THE BLESSINGS OF LIBERTY FOR OURSELVES AND OUR POSTERITY!..."

"DICK, IT'S RON REAGAN—HE WANTS TO BORROW A CUP OF ALIBIS!"

BULL

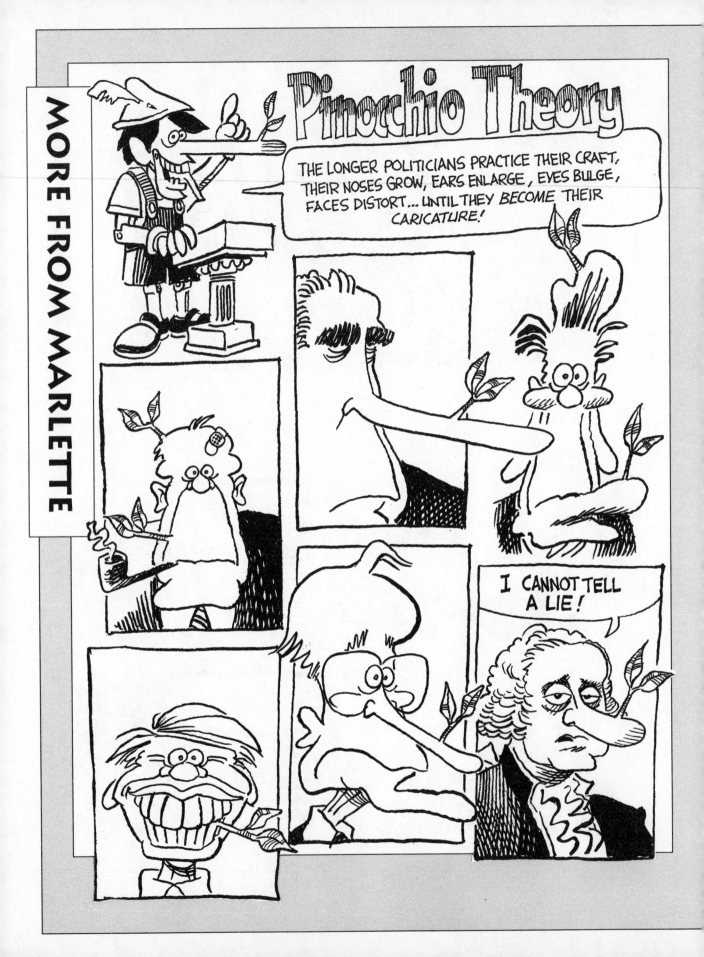

CONFESSIONS OF A STRIPPER

"**C**AN'T BE DONE," someone behind me said.

"Pardon me?" I said, looking up from the hotel guest register during an editorial cartoonists' convention.

"Can't be done!" he repeated, shaking his head. This guy was an editorial cartoonist from Denver, and several of his cronies standing nearby nodded their agreement.

"What can't be done?" I asked.

"Editorial cartoons and a comic strip both at the same time," he said, obviously referring to my daily comic strip, "Kudzu," which was being launched the next month. "One of them will have to go!"

It wasn't the first time I'd heard this. Everyone at the convention was abuzz about another editorial cartoonist who had recently attempted double duty at the drawing board and had run off to Alaska with his secretary. Word was that he had given up his editorial cartoons so he could concentrate all his energy on his strip and his wife's divorce lawyers. The message was clear: take on a comic strip and you'll end up running off to Alaska with your secretary and be forced to leave editorial cartooning.

"Too much work," the guy from Denver declared in a voice that sounded like Eeyore's in *Winnie the Pooh*. "I hope you know what you're getting yourself into."

"Oh, have you tried it?" I asked.

"No, but . . . but . . . you *can't* do both." His friends all nodded together, like the heads on those plastic puppies that bob up and down on the dashboard of a souped-up Trans Am.

"We'll see," I said. "It's worth a shot."

"Can't be done."

I had been drawing editorial cartoons for a decade when I decided to try a comic strip. At first I was intimidated by the amount of work involved. Not only did the day-to-day man-hours seem daunting on top of my full-time job as editorial cartoonist, but I also realized that a comic strip could be a lifetime commitment. That gave me pause; some of them have hung around for fifty to seventy-five years. This was like marriage; I could be wedded to the characters I created, so I'd better enjoy their company. But I was determined, and my motives were pure, simple — and ambitious. I wanted my strip to be like the ones I had loved as a child. I also wanted to find out if there was any truth to the rumor that all comic strip artists end up fabulously well-to-do.

The first thing I needed was an idea. Not only would the situation and characters have to be new and funny, it also would have to give me enough material to produce a strip a day for the rest of my life. This was about as easy as creating a new geometry theorem. The more I thought, the more convinced I became that all the good ones had been used. I hunted around and studied successful comic strips — cavemen, soldiers, kids, cats, birds, pirates, Indians, and hillbillies. They were all great, but I needed something of my own. I wanted a group of characters and a setting that was interesting and that I had some feeling about. It would have to come from my own experience. The old adage from creative writing classes, "Write what you know," seemed to apply just as much to comic strips. I began by thinking about situations that tickled me.

One thing that struck me as funny (at least now) and that I knew a lot about was being a miserable failure as a teenager. Adolescence, that awkward, off-balance time when you are no longer a child but not quite an adult, is filled with heart-breaking agony that is in turn loaded with comic potential. Humor has an intimate relationship with pain — somebody else's pain. Sitting on a whoopie cushion may be humiliating if it happens to you, but it's hilarious when it happens to someone else. All situation comedies — from "I Love Lucy" and "Leave It to Beaver" to "The Cosby Show" and "Roseanne" — are based on putting characters we identify with into horrible situations so we can watch them squirm and writhe their way out of them. No one really enjoys going through adolescence, but watching someone else's teenage years can be uproariously funny. You could say that I was an expert on this subject because my adolescence was one long, sustained whoopie cushion.

I first considered moving a small-town southerner to the wilds of New York City, setting up a fish-out-of-water situation that would naturally be full of conflict and humor. But before I got too far ahead of myself, I had to know who this guy was. I started inventing a biography for him. Where was he from? What was his hometown like, and what kind of family did he have? I had to figure this out because with all southerners you meet the family sooner or later. While exploring and fleshing out his background, I realized that where he came from was more interesting than where I was taking him. A small southern town with all the colorful eccentrics I had grown up with was just what I'd been looking for.

Late one evening I drew up a list of the town's characters with a short description of each one. I was guided in large part by my desire to get fireworks out of them. When these people

THE FIRST SKETCH AND OUTLINE OF "KUDZU" CHARACTERS

Kudzu

DUBOSE (pronounced DEW-BOWS) — INNOCENT AS THE DEW OF DIXIE MORNINGS... BRIMMING WITH DREAMS OF GLORY WHILE ONLY ONE THING STANDS IN THE WAY OF THEIR FULFILLMENT.... REALITY!

MAURICE — YOUNG, BLACK, AND A GIFT TO KUDZU... ONE OF HIS FEW LINKS TO THE REAL WORLD. MAURICE STONEWALL JACKSON (HIS ANCESTORS FOUGHT FOR THE CONFEDERACY) HAS ONE GOAL IN LIFE: TO MOVE OUT OF HIS SUBURBAN MIDDLE CLASS NEIGHBORHOOD INTO AN URBAN GHETTO.

MAMA — MRS. DUBOSE...MOTHER OF KUDZU, WIDOWED, PROUD, STRONG, WELL-BRED PATRICIAN STOCK, THOUGH NOT AS FINANCIALLY SECURE AS WAS HER FAMILY BEFORE "THE LATE UNPLEASANTNESS" (THE CIVIL WAR). WHILE UNLUCKY IN LOVE (KUDZU'S FATHER) SHE STILL HAS CULTIVATED IN HERSELF AND HER SON AN APPRECIATION FOR LIFE'S HIGHER ENDEAVORS: ART, MUSIC, LITERATURE, MOTHERHOOD.

PREACHER WILL B. DUNN — POET, PROPHET, HELLFIRE AND BRIMSTONE CLOWN, TOWN DRUNK, VILLAGE IDIOT, VILLAGE ATHEIST, RESIDENT GURU AND SELF-APPOINTED EXPERT IN "HUMAN RELATIONS."

WELCOME TO BYPASS, N.C. POP. 3,401

PLUS UNCLE DUB — RUNS THE FILLIN' STATION AND CAFE

GRANNAW DUBOSE — RUNS HER MOUTH

LAST BUT NOT LEAST.... DORIS — RUNS UP THE BIRD SEED BILL...

were placed next to each other I wanted sparks to fly. They must have been gestating in me for some time because they sprang forth full-blown, pretty much the way they remain today.

I already had the main character in mind. Kudzu is an awkward adolescent, full of ideals and poetry, who wants one thing: out. He is motivated to escape from the boring, limiting, oppressive small town he lives in. But his mother barely lets Kudzu out of her sight. Mama Dubose is so overbearing she long ago drove away her husband, which explains not only some of Kudzu's personality traits, but also why she hog-ties him to her apron strings. She is a master of manipulation, who coughs, wheezes, and is stricken with unspeakable ailments whenever Kudzu puts one foot outside the nest. Mama Dubose is southern faded gentry to his father's redneck-cracker-trailer-park gene pool. Compsons versus Snopeses.

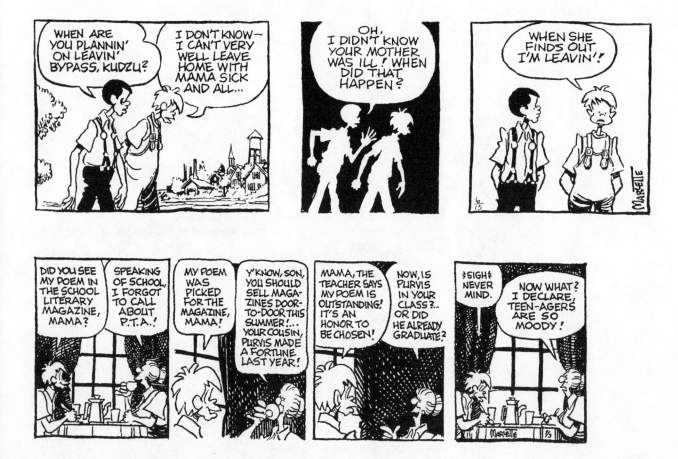

With that kind of emotional burden, Kudzu needed a friend, someone he could talk to. Enter Maurice, who is black, a skilled athlete, and about as hip and comfortable with himself as Kudzu is awkward. For all the South's notoriety regarding race relations, the reality is that blacks and whites interact more on a daily basis in the South than in other parts of the country. As a result, black-white friendships often were a natural part of growing up in small southern towns. And the racial difference between the two characters, with society's racial assumptions as a backdrop, introduces more potential for contrasts, conflict, richness, and tension.

Kudzu also had to have a love interest. Enter Veranda Tadsworth, the town beauty, the Southern Belle from Hell who has little room in her heart for anyone but Veranda. Unrequited love may be heartbreaking, but it's wide open for funny situations. Kudzu is something of an intellectual and definitely an ethereal romantic, which contrasts wonderfully with Veranda's air-headed materialism.

With Kudzu's father missing, surrogate fathers naturally came forward. Kudzu works part-time for Uncle Dub, the down-to-earth, no-nonsense filling station owner who is the Grand Old Man of the Good Ol' Boys. Uncle Dub is as concrete as Kudzu is abstract, as anti-intellectual as Kudzu is bookish, as stubborn and independent as Kudzu is reasonable and malleable, as macho as Kudzu is sensitive. A Mama's Boy like Kudzu will never be a Good Ol' Boy like Uncle Dub.

Naturally, Kudzu had to have a pet, and there was no way this kid would keep anything as mundane as a dog or a cat. My grandmother's parakeets had always fascinated me, so that's what Kudzu got. Doris is a handful. She's a party parakeet who does impressions and is addicted to chocolate. She's actually a more successful teenager than Kudzu is.

Rounding out the original cast is Reverend Will B. Dunn, Bypass's resident guru and Kudzu's spiritual guide. To my

surprise, Will B. Dunn quickly became one of the strip's most popular characters. He's based on my own Southern Baptist rearing and also to some degree on a funky preacher who married my wife and me and christened our child. Will Campbell is a self-described "bootleg preacher" without portfolio (that is, sans steeple), who, like Will B. Dunn, wears an Amish hat and cowboy boots and carries a cane. But Campbell also farms and writes novels and tends to the spiritual needs of a flock that includes radicals, Kluxers, black activists, outlaw country singers, rednecks, and cartoonists. He is a very funny man and a natural performer who does a terrific self-parody of a pompous, pious, flatulent preacher. That was most likely the real inspiration for Will B. Dunn. Some people claim that my preacher character is patterned on the real-life reverend, but Campbell goes to great lengths to deny that there's any resemblance. He has a wonderful time pointing out the differences in their hats and canes and the fact that his brand of tobacco is Beechnut while Will B. Dunn chews Red Man.

Right away Will B. Dunn developed a strong constituency — especially among the clergy — defying the conventional wisdom that a "religious" character would be too controversial and would never fly. The strip even won a Wilbur Award from the Religious Public Relations Council for portraying religion in a positive light. It is reprinted regularly in *Christian Century,* the most influential Protestant publication in the world, and in many church bulletins. I get fan letters on the Preacher's behalf from Presbyterians and Methodists, as well as Baptist ministers, Catholic priests, and Jewish rabbis. I imagine that seeing a minister in the funny papers who thinks and says the things they would like to say themselves probably relieves some of the pressure they are under to be perfect and flawless.

Over the years the strip has grown and changed. The characters venture into the outside world more now and the outside world invades Bypass more. I've also added a few new characters to the core group. Nasal T. Lardbottom, the Whitest White Boy at Bypass High and World Class Wimp, has come into his own. Mr. Goodvibes, high school guidance counselor and Village Secular Humanist, is a natural foil for Will B. Dunn. Ida Mae Wombat, geekette and future dental hygienist, has the hots for Kudzu and won't let him forget it.

It didn't take me long to discover that drawing a comic strip has about as much in common with doing a one-panel editorial cartoon as shooting a jump shot has to do with playing the violin. The two types of cartooning use entirely different creative muscles. With an editorial cartoon you have one chance, in a single frame, to tell your whole story; the punch is immediate or not at all. In a comic strip there's more time to develop an idea. The situation can unfold a bit, and with dialogue, story telling, and timing, the idea can be set up and paid off.

The audience is different for comic strips and for editorial cartoons. The editorial page reaches people who think and care about political issues, whereas comics are read by a broader audience, one that cuts across all classes and strata. My political cartoons deal with the outside world and are populated by a passing parade of characters from Washington, the State House, or City Hall. These cartoons are my reaction to the world's agenda. But "Kudzu" is more personal, dealing with more basic themes, like those eternal strivings for love, power, and chocolate. The strip and the editorial cartoons

deal with different aspects of experience, but they don't drain or take away from each other; in fact, they enhance each other.

People ask me all the time if the things that happen to Kudzu really happened to me. Yes, I was an awkward adolescent, but I never wore a chest wig like Kudzu, nor did my

mother make me carry a page beeper. Sure I had relatives like Uncle Dub, but everybody in the South does. My wife's a beauty like Veranda (and helped me figure out how the hair should look), but she's also a jock like Maurice and soaks in a bubble bath to relax like Will B. Dunn. I think all the characters reveal aspects of me and of everybody else. We all have a little of the narcissistic, self-absorbed Veranda in us. And who among us isn't a judge and moralizer, like the Preacher? Editorial cartoonists and journalists certainly are. Doris is the primitive, self-indulgent part of us. Animals are popular in comic strips because people like to see that aspect of themselves played out cutely and harmlessly. Snoopy indulges the Joe Cool/Flying Ace grandiosity that Charlie Brown denies himself, and Garfield is fat, lazy, and proud of it. We all secretly want to sleep in and pig out like a cartoon cat.

The longer I draw the "Kudzu" characters and the more familiar they get, the sharper they become. I originally named my hero "Kudzu" because I liked the way it sounded and because it had a *K* and a *z* and would be memorable. I could also imagine it on a Sunday comics page: "Kudzu," like "Steve Canyon" or "Dick Tracy." But after drawing the strip for a while, I began to see how much the character

Kudzu was like the plant he's named for. The kudzu plant was brought into the South during the Depression to help control soil erosion, but it got out of hand and now covers barns, fields, trees, and slow-moving children. It grows a foot a night and nothing can kill it. Like my character, the plant is something of a pest and is defined by its propensity to grow. The plant absorbs nutrients from its environment as does Kudzu, who is trying to take in emotional sustenance from his environment: Uncle Dub, Mama, Preacher, Veranda. Like Scarlett O'Hara or Dilsey in Faulkner's *The Sound and the Fury,* the kudzu plant — and, I hope, the comic strip — endures and prevails.

WELL, IF IT'S SUPPOSED TO BE NIXON IT CERTAINLY DOESN'T LOOK LIKE HIM

"SORRY, GENTLEMEN, BUT MR. ZIEGLER WON'T BE ENTERTAINING ANY MORE WATERGATE QUESTIONS — WILL THERE BE ANYTHING ELSE?"

AT THE HEIGHT of the Watergate scandal I drew a cartoon of Richard Nixon's press secretary, Ron Ziegler, with his tongue hanging out, tied in knots. The caption read, "Sorry, gentlemen, but Mr. Ziegler won't be entertaining any more Watergate questions — will there be anything else?"

This was during the time when John and Jim Knight, the owners of the Knight newspaper chain, were pressuring the *Charlotte Observer* to get rid of me. My editor called me into his office. Clearly the Ziegler cartoon was a last straw and it was time for a little talk.

"Y'know, son, I have always believed when it comes to cartoons the rapier works better than the sledgehammer," he began.

"Yessir," I agreed.

"And you don't go after a mosquito with an elephant gun," he added. "You use a Flit gun."

"What are you driving at, sir?"

He was obviously annoyed with me for putting him in this situation with the Knights, so as my punishment he launched into a critique of my work. As it happened, this editor had one glass eye and cataracts in the other one; he even needed a magnifying glass to read the paper. Knowing this, I couldn't really take his art criticism too seriously, but I did want to know why I was being disciplined. He pointed to the Ziegler cartoon.

"None of us is bigger than this newspaper," he concluded. "Not you. Not me. Nobody. The *Charlotte Observer* was here long before we came along, and it will be here long after we're gone."

"Yessir."

". . . and another thing. You've got to work on your caricature. That just doesn't look like Nixon," he said, pointing to the fat guy with the round nose, bald head, and horn-rimmed glasses, standing to the side of the press secretary.

"That's not supposed to be Nixon," I explained.

He grimaced, tossed the paper down, and muttered, "Well, if it was supposed to be Nixon, it certainly doesn't look like him."

I couldn't argue with that. But it just went to show: the only way to screw up a Nixon caricature was to not draw him at all.

Caricature is the art of capturing someone's likeness by exaggerating and distorting the features—a kind of overextended portraiture. The word *caricature* comes from the Italian word *caricare*, which means to load or overload. Caricature therefore is a charged portrait, a shorthand likeness that expresses the artist's feeling about the subject. If a person has big ears you make them bigger; beady eyes become beadier, a high forehead is drawn even higher, and a large nose is gigantic. Good caricature is more than the selection and distortion of features; it also involves the overall rela-

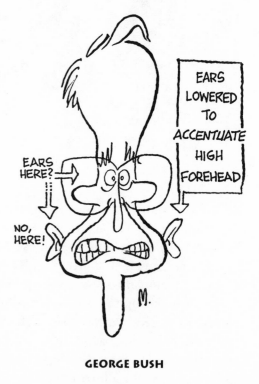

EARS HERE?

EARS LOWERED TO ACCENTUATE HIGH FOREHEAD

NO, HERE!

GEORGE BUSH

THE UGLIER YOU ARE, THE EASIER YOU ARE TO DRAW

tionship of those features to each other. Cartoonists pick and choose, and the selection is the key.

Cartoonists look for distinctive features that define the subject's face: Richard Nixon's nose, Jimmy Carter's smile, Ronald Reagan's hair. Everybody has something we can use. One of the basic rules of caricature is that the uglier your subject is, the easier he or she is to draw. And American political cartoonists have been truly blessed over the years. Lyndon Johnson had an overabundance of caricaturable features; in fact, if you put in everything you ended up with a grotesque gargoyle.

Some of us exaggerate George Bush's high narrow forehead, others concentrate on his sideways-figure-eight mouth. And though each artist's drawing may be as different from the others as a fingerprint, the results will all be recognizably George Bush.

During the Israeli invasion of Lebanon, Jewish groups said my drawings of Menachem Begin were anti-Semitic because I gave him a big nose. But I drew him that way because he *does* have a big nose. As so often happens, my caricature of him evolved; over the next few months I noticed that I was making his ears more prominent, which made his nose seem smaller. The complaints ceased.

MENACHEM BEGIN

ANTI-SEMITIC COMMENTARY
(NOSE TOO BIG)

FAIR COMMENTARY
(NOSE SAME SIZE, BUT EARS DWARF NOSE)

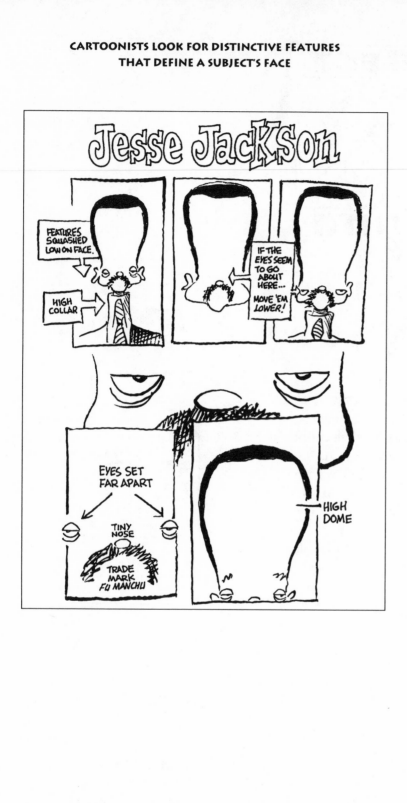

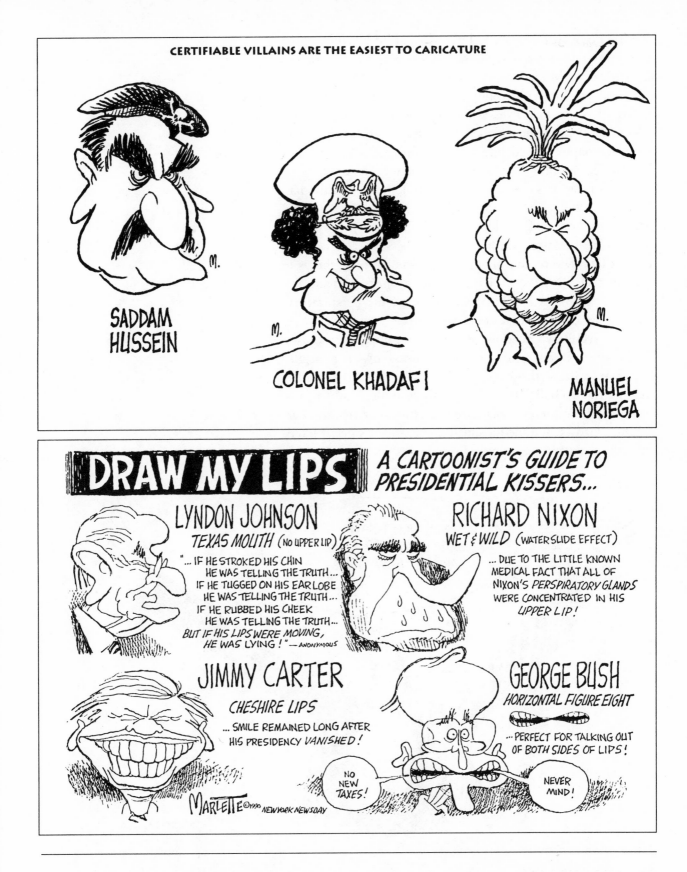

SADDAM HUSSEIN

COLONEL KHADAFI

MANUEL NORIEGA

DRAW MY LIPS *A CARTOONIST'S GUIDE TO PRESIDENTIAL KISSERS...*

LYNDON JOHNSON
TEXAS MOUTH (NO UPPER LIP)

"... IF HE STROKED HIS CHIN
HE WAS TELLING THE TRUTH...
IF HE TUGGED ON HIS EAR LOBE
HE WAS TELLING THE TRUTH...
IF HE RUBBED HIS CHEEK
HE WAS TELLING THE TRUTH...
BUT IF HIS LIPS WERE MOVING,
HE WAS LYING!" —ANONYMOUS

RICHARD NIXON
WET & WILD (WATER SLIDE EFFECT)

... DUE TO THE LITTLE KNOWN
MEDICAL FACT THAT ALL OF
NIXON'S *PERSPIRATORY GLANDS*
WERE CONCENTRATED IN HIS
UPPER LIP!

JIMMY CARTER
CHESHIRE LIPS

... SMILE REMAINED LONG AFTER
HIS PRESIDENCY *VANISHED!*

GEORGE BUSH
HORIZONTAL FIGURE EIGHT

... PERFECT FOR TALKING OUT
OF BOTH SIDES OF LIPS!

NO NEW TAXES!

NEVER MIND!

MARLETTE ©1990 NEW YORK NEWSDAY

WELL, IF IT'S SUPPOSED TO BE NIXON IT CERTAINLY DOESN'T LOOK LIKE HIM

If anybody ever complained about Richard Nixon's nose, it certainly wasn't a cartoonist. Nixon was to cartooning what Marilyn Monroe was to sex. His face was more than we could ask for. You couldn't go wrong with a caricature of him. If you got the eyes or the nose or the jowls, you had Nixon. By the time he resigned, anything a cartoonist threw down on paper looked like him. Seldom has a politician's appearance so truthfully revealed his substance. Nixon looked like his policies. His nose told you he would bomb Cambodia. The way his eyes shifted, you knew he had bugged the Democrats' national headquarters. He had the jowls of an obstructor of justice, and his face was the kind you wanted to impeach. The reason his upper lip was so long (this is a medical fact known only by a few cartoonists and the researchers at Johns Hopkins) was that all his perspiratory glands were concentrated in his upper lip.

There were two schools of thought among cartoonists about Nixon's eyes. One said you did not show them at all; you simply drew the heavy eyebrows and let the reader imagine the eyeballs lurking down there underneath. I preferred to show the eyeballs barely peeking out from under the thick brows. It added a sinisterness, and besides, I liked knowing what those eyes were up to.

YOU DON'T HAVE *DICK NIXON* TO KICK AROUND ANYMORE!

NOSE-TALGIA

RICHARD NIXON

LET'S START WITH THE EYEBROWS . . .
LIKE TWO FUZZY CATERPILLARS

THEN THE EYEBALLS . . . BARELY VISIBLE UNDER THE
EYEBROWS . . . DARTING TO HIS LEFT

THEN THE DARK CIRCLES UNDER HIS EYES

. . . THEN ADD THE NOSE . . .
THE LAST OF THE GREAT NOSES

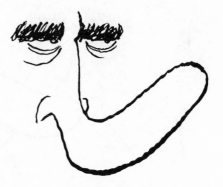

WELL, IF IT'S SUPPOSED TO BE NIXON IT CERTAINLY DOESN'T LOOK LIKE HIM

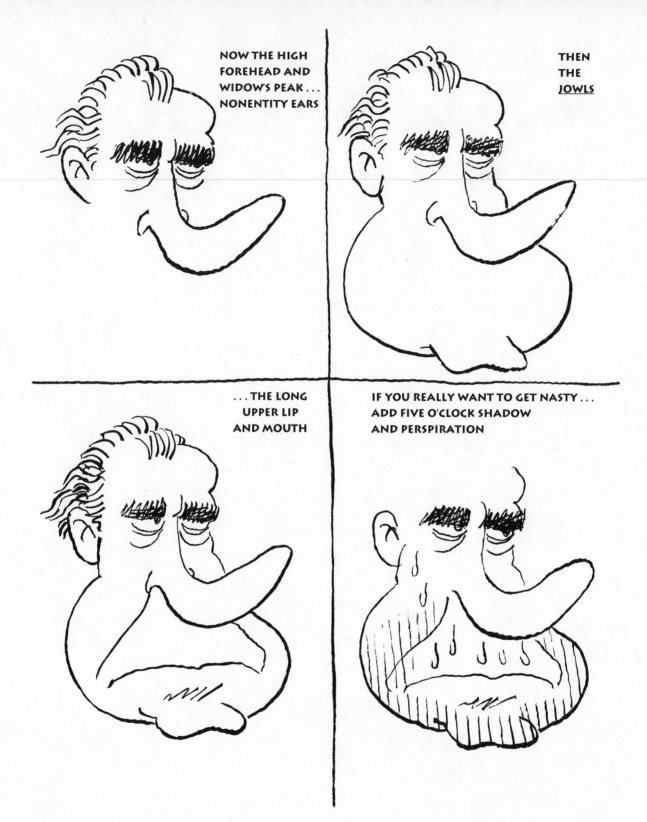

NOW THE HIGH
FOREHEAD AND
WIDOW'S PEAK...
NONENTITY EARS

THEN
THE
JOWLS

...THE LONG
UPPER LIP
AND MOUTH

IF YOU REALLY WANT TO GET NASTY...
ADD FIVE O'CLOCK SHADOW
AND PERSPIRATION

WELL, IF IT'S SUPPOSED TO BE NIXON IT CERTAINLY DOESN'T LOOK LIKE HIM

...THE SHOULDERS!

Ronald Reagan was a different story. He should have been a piece of cake, but his face was a problem to caricature because you had to do more than just capture the pompadour, the rouged cheekbones, and the protruding lower lip line. A true professional isn't satisfied with a caricature that doesn't nail the essential spirit of the man.

Cartoonists are after that certain quality that comes through despite everything the makeup artists, speechwriters, spin doctors, and press secretaries do to hide it. We're after the whole of a person's being that is greater than the sum of the parts. We're after that intangible something that lets you recognize someone walking down the beach before you can make out his features. We cartoonists are after more than the physical traits of a politician; we want his soul. The trouble was, Reagan didn't have one.

The early Reagan caricatures just didn't cut it. They showed a mean-spirited Dickensian ideologue, all wrinkles, crow's feet, and turkey neck, baring his age and his Alaric the Visigoth politics. But something was missing. These cartoons didn't jibe with the Reagan the public thought they had elected. Ronald Reagan was capable of snatching school lunches from the mouths of our children, setting James Watt loose on the environment, cutting aid to minorities, the elderly and handicapped, building more and bigger bombs, yet he still came across as . . . well . . . the Gipper. Nixon couldn't even do that. Reagan was amiable, affable, grandfatherly. Every time he gave a speech, people wanted to crawl up into his lap. Or worse, go out and vote for him. His image did not match the moral content of his policies.

The early caricatures missed this aspect of the man, and cartoonists were thrown into a tailspin of self-doubt. We were being tricked. Reagan was a decoy, a stand-in for himself. Not only was he a hands-off manager who delegated authority to his staff, he even delegated his cartoonability. His minions were the administration's mean of spirit, and they made wonderful cartoons. Watt, Meese, Abrams, et al. were Reagan's designated bullies.

But what about the president? Sometime around his visit to Bitburg it finally clicked that we weren't dealing with a traditional president, that is, a human being. What we had was a special effect. It was as if America had put something from George Lucas's Industrial Light and Magic into the White House. Capturing Reagan's essence in a drawing was

EARLY REAGAN

MEAN-SPIRITED, WRINKLED, DICKENSIAN

LATER REAGAN

...THAT LOOK OF CHEERFUL OBLIVIOUSNESS.

like trying to put your finger on a hologram. The more we drew, the more we discovered there was no *there* there.

In desperation I zeroed in on the eyes, the mirror of the soul, and finally I made it work. I gave him that look of perpetual cheerful obliviousness that has become his trademark, a kind of Zippy the Pinhead quality. Now we were cooking with gas. It was those vacant, have-a-nice-day eyes that came finally to stand for the Reagan era, and for me, nailed his caricature.

Now Ronald Reagan has ridden off into the California sunset, and of course we don't have Dick Nixon to kick around anymore, but their cartoon images are still with us, branded into our minds. When Gertrude Stein complained to Picasso that his famous portrait of her didn't look like her, the great artist told her not to worry, that in time she would resemble her portrait. In the same way, presidents end up looking more like their political cartoon caricatures than their photographs or official White House portraits.

Pinocchio's nose elongated with each falsehood he told. Likewise, the longer politicians stick around, the more their noses grow, and the bigger their ears get; their features actually distort themselves into their caricatures. Cartoonists would like to take full credit for the accuracy of our handiwork, but we can't. We have help. When the authorized biographers, presidential librarians, and other keepers of the flame who flack for former presidents write their histories and make their cases for Richard Nixon and Ronald Reagan, they'll be right about one thing. Those two definitely grew in office.

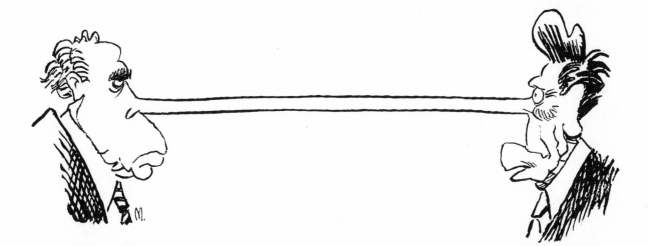

WELL, IF IT'S SUPPOSED TO BE NIXON IT CERTAINLY DOESN'T LOOK LIKE HIM

WITHOUT WORDS

ONE DAY IN JANUARY 1986 I finished my cartoon by late morning — something whimsical on NASA's space launch and the first teacher in space — and left early for lunch. On the car radio I heard the horrifying news that the space shuttle had exploded, killing all seven members of its crew. I quickly headed back to the office, hoping I would be able to come up with an image that could respond appropriately to this terrible tragedy. Soon after I got back I was told that the *Observer* was putting out a special afternoon edition on the disaster; if I wanted something in that edition I had forty-five minutes to do it. I'm not sure how it happened, but I settled immediately on a simple image of the American eagle gazing into the heavens with a single tear falling from its eye.

The drawing was in that afternoon's special edition and ran again in the next morning's paper. When I arrived at the office the following day, I found a bouquet of flowers in front of my door, left by some readers. People started calling in tears, thanking me for the drawing. The *Observer,* overwhelmed with requests for reprints, ran a notice at the bottom of the editorial page telling readers that large reproductions of my drawing were available; by ten o'clock the first morning all five hundred were gone. Another thousand were printed and were gone by 2 P.M. that same day, followed by yet another thousand that were gone by 4 P.M., even though people had to drive downtown to the *Observer* lobby to pick them up. The reprints were then made available by mail as well.

The *Observer* ended up distributing more than 70,000 prints of the drawing. Copies were sent all over the country, even to the astronauts' families and to NASA headquarters. The eagle with the teardrop hangs in homes, offices, and restaurants throughout the Carolinas. Today, years after the tragic event that inspired it, I still get requests for the drawing. Cartoonists ordinarily receive more brickbats than bouquets, but the Challenger cartoon was probably the most positively received of any I have ever drawn.

Why was there such an outpouring of emotion for this simple image? It certainly had a lot to do with the event itself which, like the assassination of President John F. Kennedy, was witnessed by the whole nation, giving it a mythic, watershed quality. But I believe the directness of the drawing and its articulation of inexpressible sorrow also played a part.

In every cartoon I try to communicate with as few words as possible. Though most cartoons need a caption to get their point across, to me the wordless ones are really special, like a hole in one in golf. My thoughts go straight into the drawing and bounce directly to the reader, with no interference. The wordless ones also give me a rush because they are rarer and tougher to bag. Whenever I pull one off, I feel like I'm hitting on all eight cylinders.

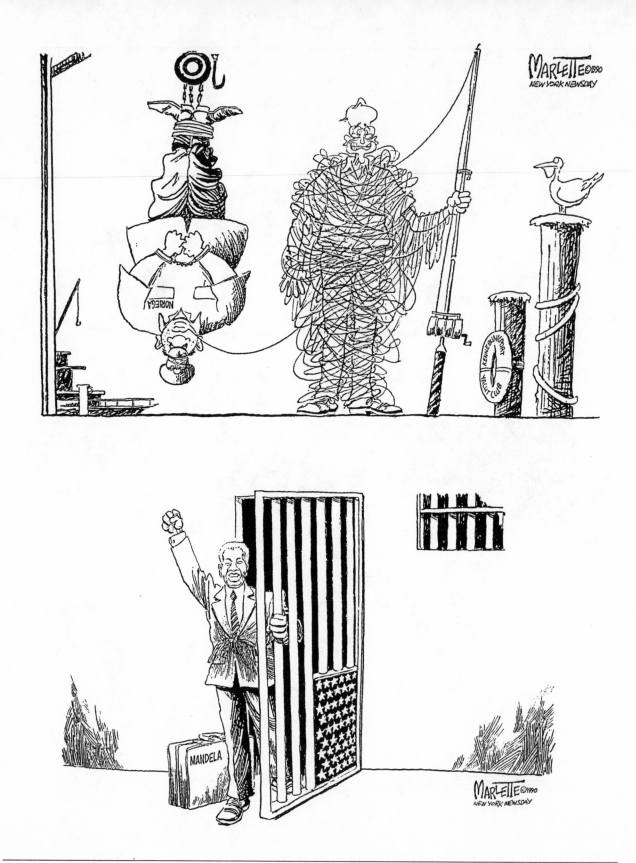

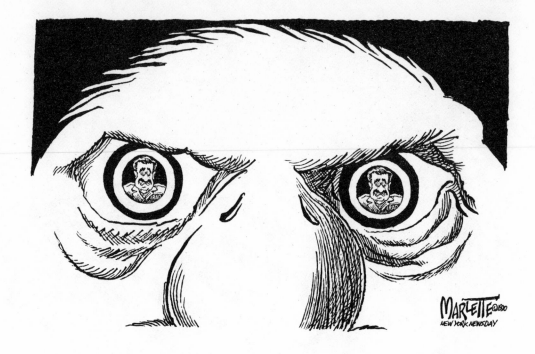

REMEMBERING
THE ORANGUTAN

I HAVE BEEN LUCKY. Having lived and drawn in several different places, I feel like the Charles Darwin of cartooning. I have studied, identified, catalogued, and classified some of the most exotic species of modern public life, from Jesse Helms and Jim and Tammy Bakker to Ted Turner, from Al Sharpton and Ed Koch to Donald Trump. It's truly been an embarrassment of riches.

These are the characters I have used for target practice. They are almost always up to something, so they are irresistible to a cartoonist. I always seem to have strong opinions about what they're doing from day to day, year to year, so I keep coming back to them as cartoon subjects. In that way I'm something like a reporter who follows a story over a long period of time. No, I'm not out there in the bushes, digging up dirt on anybody, but I often cover a story in my own way, and readers can follow it through my cartoons.

A reporter's job is to lay out the events and the facts; an editorial writer tries to convince people to see a particular point of view. My coverage of a person, event, or issue doesn't necessarily argue any side; instead I tell it like it is — or at least the way I see it. By hitting one note, one direct angle on a subject, editorial cartoons highlight and focus, helping to set an agenda for public debate.

We satirists are like elephants: we never forget. These days, if an elected official is caught in flagrante delicto with an orangutan, goes to prison,

IT'S THE ALCOHOL — I'M CHECKING INTO BETTY FORD FIRST THING TOMORROW!

blames it on drugs and alcohol, and does time at Betty Ford, all he has to do is lay low for a while, hire the right image consultant, and reelection is in the bag. A cartoonist's job is to remember —to remind ourselves and our readers of values, history, broken promises, and the orangutan.

Like heat-seeking missiles, we search out worthy targets. The bigger they are, the more powerful and corrupt, the better. Thomas Nast had Boss Tweed, Honoré Daumier had King Louis-Philippe, and Herblock owned Nixon. Just like athletes who depend on the competition to bring out their best, cartoonists need targets.

You could say that Jesse Helms and I grew up together. His first year in the United States Senate coincided with mine at the *Charlotte Observer,* which was only twenty miles from Helms's hometown. The senator is a cartoonist's dream. I noticed immediately that he was wall-eyed, like a lizard. His pupils stray away from each other, making him look like a paranoid iguana trying to see what's sneaking up behind him. All I had to do was draw horn-rimmed glasses with a single dot way off to the right side of one lens and the other one straining in the opposite direction — separate but equal, just like Jesse's racial vision.

In those early days, Helms often asked for the originals of my cartoons attacking him. Naturally I felt demoralized that a target wanted an original, but I don't think that was his intention. Politicians will take any publicity they can get, as long as their name is spelled right. Also, a shrewd politician

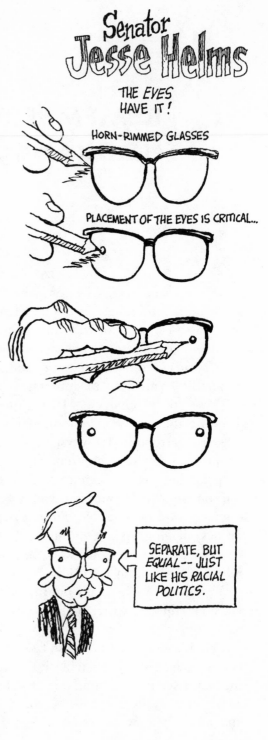

"A KID CAME UP TO ME ON THE STREET;.....SAID HE HADN'T HAD A BITE IN THREE DAYS.....SO I **BIT** HIM!....HAW! HAW! HAW!"

like Helms knows that when his constituents see a wall full of cartoons they'll say, "Look, Maude, ol' Jesse's got a sense of humor!"

Over the years, though, as my aim grew surer, his hide must have gotten thinner because Helms stopped asking for the originals and instead starting complaining to my publisher. (Democrats, I have noticed, complain to the cartoonist. Republicans go straight to the publisher.) I'm not sure which drawing pushed him over the edge, but it could have been the one of him and his colleague and clone, North Carolina's junior senator, John East, as Tweedledum and Tweedle-dummer. (I'm certain East was upset, because he called my editor and angrily explained that he was not dumb, that he was a Phi Beta Kappa with a law degree and a Ph.D. "I am not dumb," he protested. When I heard about his call, all I could say was, "I rest my case.")

Or maybe it was my drawing during Helms's assault on the Martin Luther King holiday, that suggested the senator be honored on April Fool's Day. Or perhaps it was when the

Tarheel State led the nation in turkey production and I drew Helms standing among a flock of them.

But the cartoon that generated the most negative response concerned Helms's victory over former governor Jim Hunt in the notoriously nasty 1984 U.S. Senate race, which set the standard for negative campaigning in the eighties. I drew Helms with his trousers dropped, mooning the capitol building as he smiled at the reader. The caption read: Carolina Moon Keeps Shining.

♪ ♫ CAROLINA MOON KEEPS SHINING.... ♫ ♪

This cartoon got into the paper just by the skin of its teeth. Only one editor supported it, and that was because he'd once been the Washington correspondent and had covered Jesse's mean-spiritedness up close. After a lot of debate, the decision was made to postpone the cartoon a few days. That would have landed it in the Sunday paper, but our agnostic publisher decided it was blasphemous to show the senator dropping his pants on the Sabbath, so it ran on Saturday. I was actually proud of myself for my restraint. I could have drawn Helms's backside to the reader. Now *that* would have been tasteless.

Needless to say, Helms didn't ask for the original of that one, but the switchboards lit up. His supporters were outraged by this insult to their hero during his hour of triumph. His opponents were ecstatic. The *Observer*'s Washington reporter missed the cartoon, so he was puzzled when Helms's office wouldn't return his phone calls the next day. He wanted to know whether Helms was seeking chairmanship of the Agriculture or the Foreign Relations committee. "Senator!" he shouted when he saw Helms in the hallway. "I've been trying to reach you all day! Why won't your office return my calls?"

Helms wheeled around and jabbed his finger. "You know why!"

"No, I don't. I've been out of town."

"That cartoon!" growled Helms.

"What cartoon?"

"You know which one," blustered the senator. "I'm not speaking to the *Charlotte Observer* until I get an official apology from the publisher. And you can tell him I said so."

I'm not sure if Helms ever got his apology, but I do know he was talking to our reporters the next time he wanted something in the paper.

Six years later, during the 1990 campaign, I couldn't resist drawing Helms in "Kudzu," even though I didn't live in North Carolina anymore. In the strips the senator, suffering from Cold War Separation Anxiety, was campaigning against the international artistic conspiracy — a reaction to Helms's assault on the National Endowment for the Arts. Several

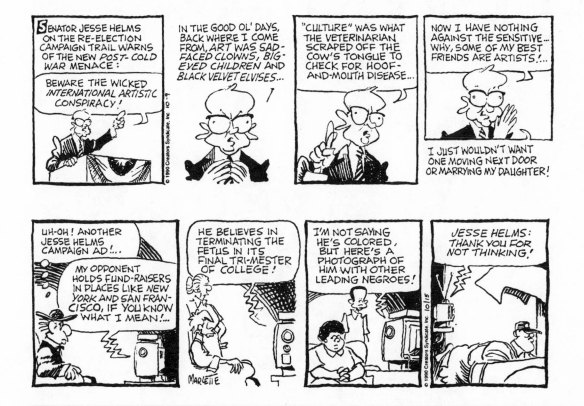

North Carolina newspapers were so concerned about my attacks on Helms that they moved "Kudzu" to the opinion pages, and the *Raleigh News and Observer* canceled it altogether. Finally hundreds of letters and telephone calls from readers forced them to reinstate it, and the paper promised to run the entire series the day after the election. Meanwhile Helms congratulated the newspapers for moving and dropping the strip, and his campaign spokesman added, "We have fought Doug Marlette's liberal point of view for years."

"IF THE LORD HAD INTENDED BLACK PEOPLE TO VOTE HE WOULDN'T HAVE MADE SO MANY OF 'EM!"

Just when I thought I'd been overly blessed with Jesse Helms, along came Jim and Tammy Bakker and the PTL Club. My cup runneth over. The *Charlotte Observer* was the Bakkers' local newspaper, which made me their hometown cartoonist. Jesse Helms may have made my day, but Jim and Tammy changed my life.

One of the first PTL cartoons I drew — ten years before Bakker resigned — was about an abrupt and unceremonious canning of a portion of his staff. The drawing showed Bakker as Christ at the Last Supper telling his disciples: "I don't know how to break this to you, but I'm afraid I'm going to have to let some of you go!" Bakker's aides claimed that Jim was on his knees weeping into the shag carpeting over the cartoon. I didn't feel overly troubled by his reaction, though, because a weeping Jim Bakker hardly indicated serious emotional trauma. If you watched the Bakkers' TV show, you knew Jim and Tammy could burst into tears over anything from lost souls to burnt toast.

When Jim confessed that he'd been messing around with church secretary Jessica Hahn, and resigned in disgrace, the nation and the world discovered what we in Charlotte had been covering for more than a decade — the water slides, the

crystal palaces, Tammy Faye's shopping demons, the malfeasance and mismanagement, the carnival of tacky excess that was the PTL. I once drew a Jordan River baptismal scene with Bakker wearing a rubber-ducky inner tube and careening off a water slide over the heads of a startled Jesus and John the Baptist.

When free-sex guru Bhagwan Rajneesh was arrested in Charlotte I responded with a cartoon of the Bhagwan and Bakker, each driving a Rolls Royce, in a head-on collision on a Charlotte street. That one particularly outraged PTL executives.

In my early days of PTL cartooning, just about anything provoked a strong negative reaction from the Bakkers' ardent admirers. Jim and Tammy even held up my cartoons on their TV show, denouncing them as "tools of Satan." Their followers were encouraged to protest with phone calls, letters, and subscription cancellations.

"You're a tool of Satan!" a caller screamed when I answered the office phone once.

"Excuse me?"

"You're a tool of Satan!"

"I'm sorry, but that's impossible," I said.

"What?" asked the caller.

"I can't be a tool of Satan," I said. "Our personnel department tests us for that sort of thing."

"What?"

"Knight-Ridder newspapers have a strict policy against hiring tools of Satan," I explained and hung up.

Someone actually sent me a tape recording of a sermon preached against me and my cartoons at a Baptist church less than a mile from my home. The death threats came later.

When Jerry Falwell replaced Bakker, I drew a cartoon of Mr. Moral Majority as a snake in the PTL paradise saying, "Jim and Tammy were expelled from paradise and left me in charge!" That cartoon drove the beleaguered PTLers even crazier because Falwell was being hailed as a white knight rescuing the ministry of his fallen brethren. The Reverend Richard Dortch (now defrocked and serving time) showed the cartoon on the air and said, "The real target is not Jim and Tammy Bakker. It isn't Richard Dortch. It isn't Jerry Falwell. It's God's work." The audience wept and sang.

"THAT'S RIGHT — JIM AND TAMMY WERE EXPELLED FROM PARADISE AND LEFT ME IN CHARGE!"

Falwell and his minions loudly demanded that our publisher, editors, reporters, and I apologize publicly. To all angry callers and grumbling editors I responded, "There is a lot of precedent in the New Testament for referring to religious professionals as snakes. Jesus called the Pharisees, the spokesmen for the Moral Majority of His time, a 'brood of vipers.' John the Baptist and the Old Testament prophets were even less genteel." Some editors and reporters at the paper didn't like that drawing because Falwell was the primary source for the dirt they were getting on Bakker — sex rumors, funny money, and homosexuality — and my cartoon had alienated their source.

During his trial Jim Bakker crawled into a fetal position beneath his lawyer's couch and was carted off to the loony bin. Some people thought he was faking, but I wasn't surprised. Jim Bakker was always in the fetal position, totally helpless and dependent. Under his attorney's sofa or on top of the world, it didn't matter. He played the helpless little boy in trouble who counted on daddy to bail him out — whether dad was a new accountant, a new lawyer, Jerry Falwell, or Jahweh himself.

I marveled at the Bakkers' consistency over the years;

through all their trials and tribulations they hardly changed a bit and never seemed to learn a thing. But what shelf life! What staying power! In a culture that devours celebrities every fifteen minutes (ask Judy Carne and Erik Estrada), Jim and Tammy were masters at holding the public eye. "What's the difference between Jim and Tammy and the common cold?" one of my cartoons once asked. "Sooner or later a cold goes away." Celebrities were once people who ran the fastest mile, created the greatest painting, climbed the highest mountain. Today they compete to have the biggest divorce settlement, the worst drug habit, or the longest prison sentence.

All along, Bakker's religion was less about devotion to the God of Abraham, Isaac, and Jacob than to devotion to the cult of Me, Myself, and Mine. Jim and Tammy were prophets, role models, and martyrs to the one true religion of this age, the Cult of Narcissus.

" HI !... DO YOU KNOW ME ?..."

" RELAX—IT'S JUST JIM AND TAMMY COMING AGAIN!"

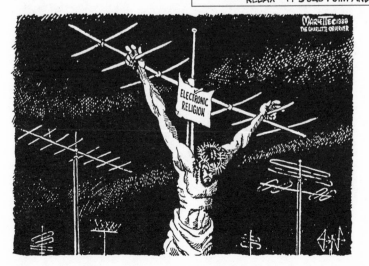

When I moved to New York City it was like landing in a cartoonist's brier patch. New York's politicians and personalities are already so much larger than life that a cartoonist's job is almost too easy. Some of my first cartoons for *Newsday* were of Ed Koch's run for reelection after twelve years as mayor. Even though he lost, I was glad I got to draw him during the campaign. Koch *was* New York City. His brash, tough-guy stance caught the spirit of the city. When my editor introduced me to Koch as the paper's new cartoonist, he looked at me with all the warmth of a pit bull. His eyes had the wariness that New Yorkers learn to take with them on the streets and in the subways.

Koch is an anachronism today. Whereas most politicians hire professionals to tailor and stage-manage their public image, Koch is his own spin doctor. He doesn't walk on pins and needles to avoid controversy the way most politicians do; he is a bull in a china shop. Somewhere he learned to speak fluent "tabloid headline" and "sound bite," and, like the nerdy teenager who suddenly discovers he can hit a jump shot, he does it all the time. A politician who writes your cartoon captions is very helpful.

Only in New York City would a candidate declare his sexual preference during the heat of a mayoral campaign. Koch announced that he was not gay just as if he were stating his position on a bond issue. He was then being questioned about his involvement in a patronage scam called the Talent Bank. I drew him wearing a Talent Bank button, his body a crooked cacophony of jutting angles, bends, and distortions. The caption balloon said, ". . . but sexually I'm straight!"

The longer Koch stayed in office, the more he grew into his caricature. His features are generous — prominent nose, beady eyes, bald head, frizzy fringe of hair. The feisty attitude, the smug smile, the crocodile-tear sentimentality, the street-smart savvy all made him an irresistible, classic cartoon target. When David Dinkins won in the primary, I drew Koch knocked flat on his back in a boxing ring, mouthing his infamous "How am I doing?"

In New York I feel less like a cartoonist than a documentarian. Something about this city produces personalities that speak to the ultimate symptoms of our age. My targets in New York are more than buffoons and charlatans; they are bacilli of the spiritual diseases plaguing the latter part of the twentieth century. Like Koch, they are paradigms — walking, talking cartoons.

• Donald Trump is Midas. He embodies the crass acquisitiveness, naked aggression, and narcissism of the self-absorbed Reagan era. At first everything he touches turns to gold; later it turns to fecal matter.

" THERE'S SOMEONE ELSE, ISN'T THERE, DONALD?! "

• Leona Helmsley is the wicked witch of the west.

• Al Sharpton is the Reverend Bacon from *The Bonfire of the Vanities*.

- John Gotti is a two-bit Michael Corleone from *The Godfather*.
- Michael Millken is Gordon Gekko, the demigod of greed in the movie *Wall Street*.
- Mario Cuomo is Hamlet: "To run or not to run."

"THAT DOES IT!... I'VE GOT TO DO SOMETHING ABOUT CRIME IN THE STREETS!"

The list goes on and on. Every day they all dare me to draw them. A cartoonist in this city has as many potential targets as a mugger in the streets. The question becomes: If you're the child in the fairy tale who points out that the emperor has no clothes, what happens when you find yourself living in a nudist colony?

I sometimes wonder how New York's Thomas Nast, the father of American editorial cartooning, would choose his targets if he were drawing "them damned pictures" in the Naked City today.

A KUDZU SAMPLER

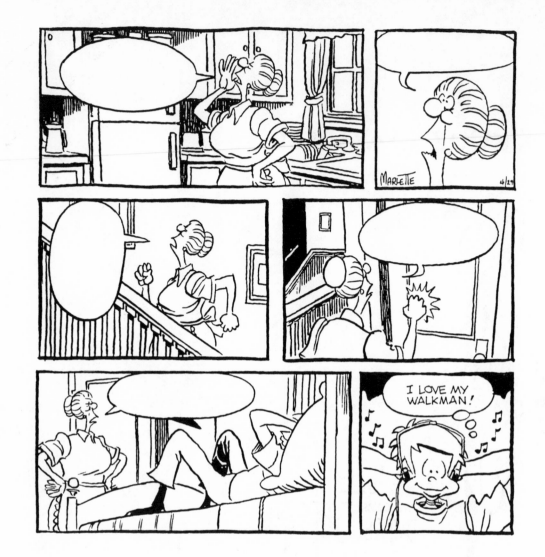

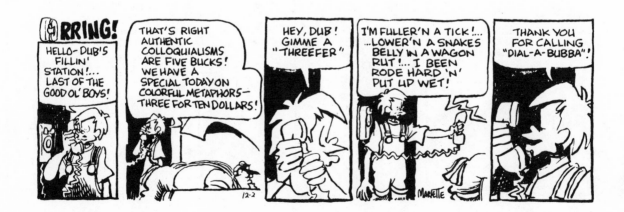

SURVIVORS

BENJAMIN FRANKLIN once observed that houseguests are like fish; after three days they start to smell. He could just as easily have been talking about most political cartoons, which, along with newspaper columns, have almost no shelf life. What for a moment seemed witty and acerbic, reflecting brilliantly the time we live in, becomes quickly anachronistic as the public's attention moves on to other issues.

Ironically, the stronger the cartoon — naming specific names, playing off the subtleties of the issues and exploring the quirkiness of the personalities involved — the more likely it is to die a quick and horrible death. Seldom do you hear someone at a cocktail party say, "Remember that fabulous cartoon on Ann Gorsuch's mess at the EPA?"

Sometimes when I am asked to address a crowd of unsuspecting people, many of whom believe that cartoonists, like children and novelists, are best seen and not heard, I show slides of my work to draw attention away from the spectacle of my tongue making a fool of me. I regularly update my slide show with cartoons on the latest hot topics. But what fascinates me are those cartoons that have settled into a permanent place in the carousel because they have not been dimmed by time or by shifts in public taste and interests. Audiences continue to respond to them, and they remain as fresh today as when they were first drawn. I call them the survivors, the evergreens, the perennials. Here are a few of my favorites.

"DON'T BLAME ME—YOU'RE THE ONE WHO INSISTED ON A FROZEN EMBRYO!..."

"AS, LIKE, CLASS VALEDICTORIAN, YOU KNOW, I WAS TRYING TO THINK, YOU KNOW, IN MY HEAD, LIKE, WHAT TO SAY AND JUNK.....AND, YOU KNOW, LIKE IT'S REALLY WEIRD BUT TWELVE YEARS OF PUBLIC EDUCATION — I MEAN, WHOA!.....ANYWAY, THAT'S WHAT I THINK IN MY HEAD, YOU KNOW?"

"HOT DANG, EDNA—I GOT ME A SECULAR HUMANIST!"

"REMEMBER WHEN THEY USED TO SEND US POVERTY PROGRAMS!..."

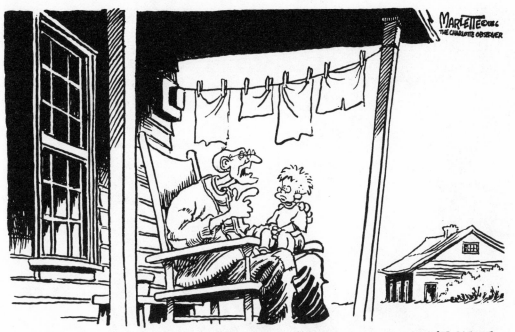

"WHY, WHEN I WAS A BOY WE WERE SO BAD OFF WE DIDN'T HAVE A SINGLE CELEBRITY INTERESTED IN OUR PLIGHT!"

"TAKE TWO ASPIRIN AND SUE ME IN THE MORNING!"

"PRESIDENT?... NO, CHILD, BUT YOU CAN GROW UP TO BE FRONT-RUNNER!"

" I TOLD YOU FLORIDA NEVER SHOULD
HAVE RELAXED ITS GUN LAWS!..."

"I'M GONNA PASS THE TOYOTA, HONEY— COVER ME!"

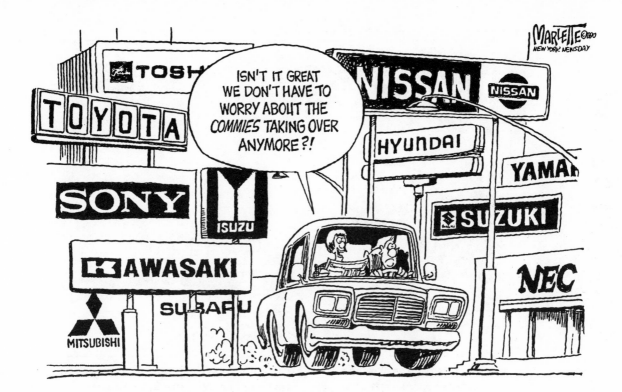

THIS OBITUARY CARTOON FOR CIA DIRECTOR WILLIAM CASEY WAS PULLED BY THE
ATLANTA CONSTITUTION'S EDITORIAL PAGE EDITOR. HE SAID IT MADE
FUN OF THE DEAD, WHO CAN'T DEFEND THEMSELVES.

NEWSDAY EDITORS CLAIMED THAT THIS CARTOON, DRAWN WHEN JIM BAKKER WAS SENT TO PRISON,
WAS RACIST BECAUSE IT USED THE NAME BIG LEROY. I ARGUED THAT THE WHITE LEROYS I KNEW PROB-
ABLY OUTNUMBERED THE BLACK LEROYS THEY KNEW, BUT THEY REMAINED UNPERSUADED. I REFUSED
TO CHANGE THE WORDING OF BAKKER'S LETTER BECAUSE I FELT IT WOULD BE WRONG AND SILLY, SO THE
CARTOON NEVER RAN ON THE EDITORIAL PAGES.

THE ONES THEY WOULDN'T PRINT

THE BEST CARTOONS make people uncomfortable — especially editors and publishers.

The first time an editor got seriously squeamish over one of my cartoons was right after I left the anything-goes world of college journalism and entered the "real" world of daily newspapering. I was working in the art department of the *St. Petersburg Times* and occasionally contributing an editorial cartoon. A controversy over school desegration had exploded at one of the high schools. The students went by the nickname "Rebels," flew the Confederate Stars and Bars, and played "Dixie" at football games. The newly bused-in black students protested these customs, which stirred up white resentment, resulting in violence on campus. The media and the community were whipping themselves into a frenzy.

I was driving my Volkswagen home from work one day when a cartoon idea struck me and nearly ran me off the road. In it a couple of high school students are flying a swastika-emblazoned flag at a pep rally. One says, "I just don't understand why those Jewish kids are so uptight about our school flag." It was my first cartoon on a controversial local issue for a major metropolitan daily, and it hit the bullseye. I felt like I had caught lightning in a bottle. I was almost hyperventilating by the time I sat

"I JUST DON'T UNDERSTAND WHY THOSE JEWISH KIDS ARE SO UPTIGHT ABOUT OUR SCHOOL FLAG!"

down to draw it, and my hands were shaking so much I could barely control my brush.

The cartoon never ran. The editors agreed with the point I was making, but they worried that it would only fuel an already volatile situation. My cartoons ran only at the indulgence of the editorial page editor, so I was hardly in a position to argue. I had to let it go at that.

Since then my cartoons have prompted a lot of "to run or not to run" discussions. During my first year in Charlotte I was the subject of numerous letters to the editor. It would start with an avalanche of letters against a cartoon and that would ignite readers to my defense. Petitions to get me fired prompted others supporting me. Readers either loved the cartoons or hated them, but they didn't ignore them. The head of the local electric utility, the mighty Duke Power Company's Bill Lee, didn't like my cartoons that were critical of nuclear power. He even drew his own cartoon for publication; in a completely black panel, two eyes stared out at the reader, with the caption "Marlette drawing cartoons without nuclear energy."

MARLETTE DRAWING CARTOONS WITHOUT NUCLEAR ENERGY
(by Bill Lee of Duke Power)

The chairman of the Mecklenburg County school board, Bill Poe, complained to an *Observer* reporter about a cartoon that said he had dragged his feet on desegregation. "What rock did he [Marlette] crawl out from under?" he asked. County Commissioner Bob Walton wrote a letter to the editor denouncing a cartoon that showed ex-banker Luther Hodges holding up his own bank to pay off his campaign debt after defeat in the U.S. Senate primary race. "This cartoon is a damn disgrace," Walton wrote. "What was the purpose or intent? This is journalism at its worst. . . ." When editor David Lawrence passed on Walton's comments to the person who should have been most offended by my drawing, Hodges responded, "I have no problem with the cartoon. I do indeed have debt problems!" Early in the Reagan years a group of prominent local business and civic leaders urged *Charlotte Observer* editor Rich Oppel to fire me because, as they explained, the nation had reached a critical juncture with the election of Ronald Reagan, and the Marlette cartoons were, in their words, "a threat to civilization."

Charlotte proudly calls itself the "most churched" city in America, and televangelists such as Jim and Tammy Bakker set up their empires nearby. Since I was living in a community that took its religion seriously, I tried to follow suit with my cartoons. Early on I began celebrating Good Friday with drawings that recast Christian symbols and meanings to make them apply to modern social problems. The cartoons were controversial, but the paper let them run — at first. I started with a cartoon about the debate over amnesty for draft resisters. In it a child holding a Bible explains to another, ". . . but even though they believed in the death penalty and killed Him, He believed in amnesty and forgave them, and that's why it's called Good Friday."

"....BUT EVEN THOUGH THEY BELIEVED IN CAPITAL PUNISHMENT AND KILLED HIM HE BELIEVED IN AMNESTY AND FORGAVE THEM, AND THAT'S WHY IT'S CALLED 'GOOD FRIDAY.'....."

Another of my Good Friday cartoons was about an escalation in the U.S. bombings in Southeast Asia. I drew a line of Vietnamese refugees in silhouette, fleeing the destruction; among them was Christ bearing the cross. These cartoons became such a tradition and generated so much flak that the

editors of the *Observer* started dreading Good Friday months ahead, as if they were going to Calvary themselves.

One of the Good Friday cartoons was censored from the paper. At that time North Carolina led the nation in the number of prisoners on Death Row, and I drew Christ with an electric chair on his back marching up Golgotha. When David Lawrence refused to run it, he set off an uproar in the newsroom. People debated the meaning of the cartoon as well as what the whole thing said about the right of free expression. Lawrence ended up writing a column that tried to justify killing the cartoon; ironically, he ran the suppressed cartoon with the column.

Most of the trouble I have run into over biblical or religious imagery in my cartoons has come not from believers but from secular humanists. The doubts, fears, and gnashing of teeth always have come from those who either had no particular religious affiliation or were avowed agnostics. Editors who count themselves among the faithful have usually seen that my cartoons are theologically sound and have had no problem with them.

Back when the infamous PTL scandal was still a local story for the *Charlotte Observer,* we drew a lot of heat from PTL supporters. As a play on our reporting of the story, I drew a cartoon inspired by Leonardo da Vinci's *Last Supper;* Jim Bakker sits in the middle saying, "One of you shall betray me!" while at the end of the table an *Observer* reporter sits smiling mischievously as he furiously takes notes.

The newspaper's publisher, Rolfe Neill, squelched the cartoon when he spotted it on the page layout. He said he was worried it gave evidence to the charge that the paper had a vendetta against PTL. By this point the *Observer* had become part of the story; the cartoon was my way of poking fun at us, not at PTL. I tried to persuade Neill that the

" ...ONE OF YOU SHALL BETRAY ME."

cartoon shouldn't be held hostage to institutional public relations concerns and that it would help defuse tensions by showing that we could laugh at ourselves. He never went for it, proving that, indeed, we couldn't laugh at ourselves. It wasn't just the PTL connection that bothered him; some editors and publishers find overtly religious subject matter just too hot to handle.

Later, when I was at *Newsday,* a group of Catholic prelates advocated withholding communion from politicians who didn't toe the anti-abortion line. I drew Christ and the apostles from Leonardo da Vinci's *Last Supper* seated under a sign that said, "No Shirt, No Socks, No Pro-life, No Service." An editor at the paper, a lapsed Catholic, scotched that cartoon, declaring with the certainty of an ex cathedra papal proclamation that it "makes fun of religion." I argued both times that Leonardo's painting was not the same as the event itself. To treat a painting, no matter what it depicts, as holy or sacred is idolatry and strictly prohibited in the scriptures. There is a tendency for the literal-minded, whether they are biblical literalists or secular humanist journalists, to mistake a sign for what it points to.

When New York's Cardinal John O'Connor hired a public relations firm to bolster the church's worldly image vis-à-vis the abortion issue, I drew a couple of Roman soldiers at the Crucifixion, one saying to the other, "He should've hired

" HE SHOULD'VE HIRED A GOOD *P.R. FIRM!* "

UNACCEPTABLE

a good P.R. firm." After heated exchanges, my editor refused to run it because he said it was blasphemous. But I was determined to comment on O'Connor's new P.R. flacks, and a few days later I came up with a cartoon that the paper found acceptable. One bishop says to a colleague, "No, *you* tell 'em we hired another firm," as they pass a door inscribed, "Matthew, Mark, Luke, and John, Public Relations."

Rarely have I clashed with an editor because of political differences. I have been lucky enough to work with newspaper editors who share my political values and who are ardent supporters of free expression. Still, emotionally charged issues like Israel's 1982 invasion of Lebanon or the Palestinian uprising can bring out

" NO, *YOU* TELL 'EM WE HIRED ANOTHER FIRM! "

ACCEPTABLE

the most irrational responses from readers and editors alike. One editor I know at a Cox newspaper prohibited his cartoonist from using the Star of David, even when drawing Israeli tanks, which happen to have the Star of David on their sides. A cartoon I drew on Israel's suppression of the Palestinian uprising prompted the Emory University bookstore to cancel a book signing because they had received threats of protests and demonstrations if I appeared. The cartoon, one of the most controversial of my career, showed Israeli soldiers bursting through a garret door and finding a young girl scribbling in her diary. "Anne Frank!" they gasped.

I never draw a cartoon that doesn't have a good shot at running in the paper. And most of the time they do. But when they crash and burn it's more often over a question of taste than because of politics. For instance, when Reagan's attorney general, Ed Meese, called for mandatory drug testing in the workplace, I saw this as a perfect opportunity to nail him for his cavalier disregard for civil liberties. I drew him with his back to the reader, facing the Bill of Rights; Reagan was next to him, holding a beaker and saying, "No, Meese — the urine sample goes in here!" The *Observer* felt the cartoon was in bad taste and killed it right before publication. I thought it was entirely appropriate. I wasn't the one who introduced urine samples into public discourse; Ronald Reagan did that.

"ANNE FRANK!"

" NO, MEESE—THE URINE SAMPLE GOES IN HERE!"

But since the subject was out there, I thought my cartoon handled an inelegant topic legitimately and on target. Memos flew. But before it was resolved, the editor fled on a trip to China; by the time he returned, the cartoon was no longer timely.

I don't begin each day trying to tick people off. It is no great skill or talent to offend. I even avoid profanity in my cartoons, because it always alienates some people. Don't get me wrong. I don't mind cartoons that offend people, as long as it's for the right reasons. Cartoonists are responsible for keeping readers awake. Part of our marching orders is to find startling and provocative ways of expressing things. But because our job requires us to push the boundaries, it's inevitable that we'll cross the line now and then. Naturally our sense of taste and acceptability differs from an editor's — and it should. One of the reasons they hire us is that we don't think like them. After all, taste resides in the mouth of the beholder, and as Jesse Helms and the Ayatollah Khomeini have taught us, one man's art is another man's bad breath.

The miracle, I suppose, is that pungent cartoons are tolerated in newspapers at all. Their realm is that of images and dreams. The best cartoons are wild fanatical creatures of the heart that cannot be tamed or made to submit to the controls of objective journalism without breaking their spirit and robbing them of their power.

Nobody understands the adage "Freedom of the press belongs to the person who owns one" better than cartoonists. We are the point men, the mine sweepers for free speech. What do I think when a cartoon is pulled? It's their newspaper, they can run whatever they want. The ones they wouldn't print? I can deal with that. The ones I would stop myself from drawing . . . now that's scary.

"SORRY, BEN . . . NICE CARTOON, BUT KING GEORGE MAY BE OFFENDED."

FOR WHOM THE CARTOON TOLLS

WHEN CARTOONISTS draw obituary cartoons, we sometimes call them "that Great Cartoon in the Sky." The most obvious way of doing them is to show St. Peter greeting the deceased at the Pearly Gates. My first obit cartoon was of Jack Benny entering the gates of heaven with a Brinks truck. St. Peter said, "Sorry, sir, rules are rules. You can't take it with you." A lot of readers were touched, but others thought I was making fun of the dead. You could say it was my introduction to how sensitive readers can be about cartoons.

Over time I discovered an unwritten rule about obit cartoons: never make light of the dead — unless it's a dead communist. When Mao Tse-Tung died, I drew a casket with an empty thought balloon over it; the caption read, "The Thoughts of Chairman Mao." Leonid Brezhnev invaded heaven in a tank. It turned out that I could have drawn these guys burning in hell and nobody would have uttered a peep. After all, they were Commies.

The legendary Ding Darling drew his own obit cartoon. In it, a ghostly figure tips his hat as he checks out of his office. The walls are covered with classic Ding cartoons, and there's a drawing board and an empty chair. The caption reads, "Bye, now. It's been wonderful knowing you." Darling drew the cartoon three years before he died and gave his secretary strict orders to run it the day after his death. So far I've avoided drawing my own obituary; it was hard enough making out a will.

"BREZHNEV!"

HE'S HERE!

HOW SWEET IT WAS

LUCY IN THE SKY WITH DIAMONDS

TREASURE OF THE SIERRA MADRES

TOP HAT

Shortly after the fall of Communism in Eastern Europe, I found myself scarfing up good old American hot dogs at a Fourth of July weenie roast at the United States Embassy in Prague. It was the first Independence Day celebrated in that part of the world in quite some time, so the festivities, presided over by Ambassador Shirley Temple Black, were especially giddy and euphoric. President Vaclav Havel showed up, as did other distinguished Czech dignitaries and some of the most luminescent names in American journalism. The first, historic East-West Journalism Conference was being held in Prague that week, organized by Bill Kovach of the Nieman Foundation at Harvard University and Tom Winship of the Center for Foreign Journalists; the visiting newsmen and newswomen had been invited to Shirley's for a picnic. That week journalists from both sides of the rapidly disappearing Iron Curtain gathered to discuss the problems of a free press and of covering elections, and the issue of transition from government control to an open exchange of ideas and information in Eastern Europe and the Soviet Union. I filed this cartoon report from Prague.

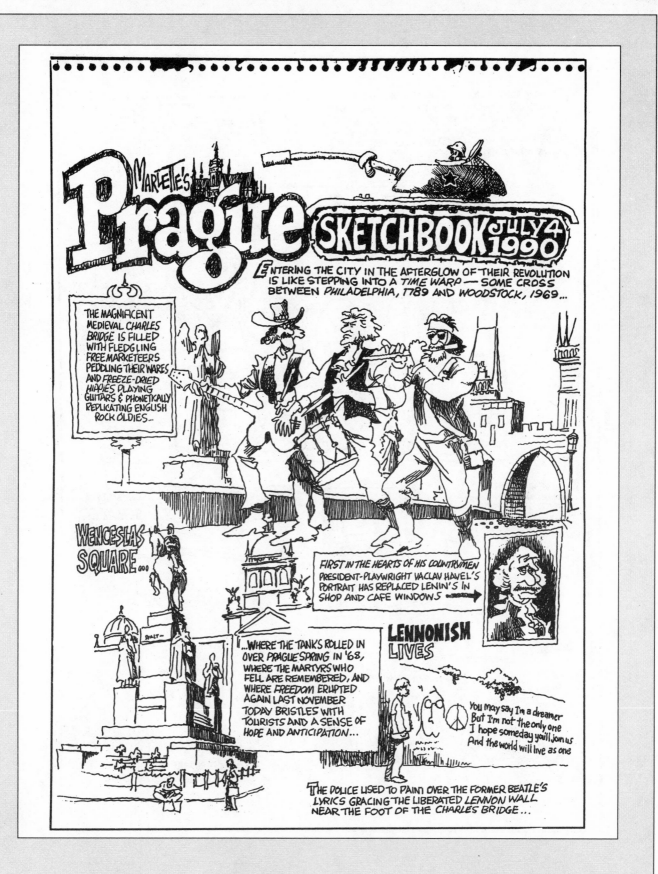

MARLETTE'S **Prague** SKETCHBOOK JULY 4 1990

ENTERING THE CITY IN THE AFTERGLOW OF THEIR REVOLUTION IS LIKE STEPPING INTO A *TIME WARP* — SOME CROSS BETWEEN *PHILADELPHIA, 1789* AND *WOODSTOCK, 1969...*

THE MAGNIFICENT MEDIEVAL *CHARLES BRIDGE* IS FILLED WITH FLEDGLING FREE-MARKETEERS PEDDLING THEIR WARES AND *FREEZE-DRIED HIPPIES* PLAYING GUITARS & PHONETICALLY REPLICATING ENGLISH ROCK OLDIES...

WENCESLAS SQUARE...

FIRST IN THE HEARTS OF HIS COUNTRYMEN PRESIDENT-PLAYWRIGHT *VACLAV HAVEL'S* PORTRAIT HAS REPLACED *LENIN'S* IN SHOP AND CAFE WINDOWS

...WHERE THE TANKS ROLLED IN OVER *PRAGUE SPRING* IN '68, WHERE THE MARTYRS WHO FELL ARE REMEMBERED, AND WHERE *FREEDOM* ERUPTED AGAIN LAST NOVEMBER TODAY BRISTLES WITH TOURISTS AND A SENSE OF HOPE AND ANTICIPATION...

LENNONISM LIVES

You may say I'm a dreamer
But I'm not the only one
I hope someday you'll join us
And the world will live as one

THE POLICE USED TO PAINT OVER THE FORMER BEATLE'S LYRICS GRACING THE LIBERATED *LENNON WALL* NEAR THE FOOT OF THE *CHARLES BRIDGE*...

HOW DO YOU GET YOUR IDEAS?

THE QUESTION I'M ASKED most often — even more than "Is that all you do?" — is "How do you get your ideas?" It's also the hardest to answer because my methods and sources are extremely varied, and the process is difficult to pin down. I never know when or where I'll be hit with a cartoon idea. One day I had just wrapped up my editorial cartoon and was in a hurry to get home to ink some dailies for my strip and mail them off that evening. I scampered out of the office and crossed the street to the uptown subway. Deadlines always put me into a frenzy of production and pump my adrenalin.

Luckily (for a change), a train was just pulling in. Maybe I can get this done after all, I thought. Sitting down, my mind started working on the strips I had to complete. I glanced up at the ad posters across the car, and there was a tuxedoed Jerry Lewis smiling down at me to promote his Labor Day telethon. This was just a month or so after Iraq had invaded Kuwait, and Saddam Hussein had been posing with children for the world's television cameras. As I stared at the poster an idea came to me. Jerry's Kids . . . Labor Day Telethon . . . Saddam's Kids.

At the next stop I switched to the downtown train and headed back to the office. I spent that short ride calculating how much time it would take to draw the cartoon, whether the one I had already done could be held a day, and if I could still get the strips into Federal Express that night. At the same time I was refining the Saddam's Kids idea. After some back and forth with myself, I drew Hussein holding a gun to

I DON'T HEAR THOSE PHONES RINGING!

Saddam's KIDS

Labor Day TELETHON

MARLETTE ©1990
NEW YORK NEWSDAY

the head of a frightened child, saying with a menacing smile, "I don't hear those phones ringing."

A cartoonist must develop an openness to suggestion and a willingness to change direction on a dime. I was not looking for an idea, nor was I thinking about the Iraq situation. In fact, I was preoccupied with other problems. The connection between Hussein's unctuous concern for the kids and Jerry Lewis's smiling face happened unconsciously. But years of practice trains a cartoonist to be a sponge, to make visual associations and recognize connections. The Saddam's Kids idea made me giddy with delight and wonder. I thought it had just the right kind of irony and made its point. It seemed like magic, even to me. It's more than that, though; a sudden idea is actually a product of practice, discipline, and hard work.

So how do I get ideas?

First I have a gut reaction or instinctive take on a situation. I ask myself, what do I want to say? Then I try to find a visual metaphor that sums up the idea, a this-is-like-that. It's a kind of channeled free association in which I roam free, guided always by what I want to say. I jot down words and phrases, and I sketch and doodle until something clicks. The best cartoon ideas sneak up on you and often cannot be traced back to their origins. Once, while doggedly stalking the Lithuanian secession, I ended up with something on the baseball lockout.

I sometimes start with a general idea and narrow it down until it's specific. For instance, the Equal Rights Amendment

FIRST I HAVE A GUT REACTION

naturally brought to mind classic battle-of-the-sexes situations—husbands and wives, brides and grooms. I wanted to draw a cartoon about the disparity between a man's earning a dollar to a woman's fifty-nine cents. I started with Adam and Eve, which led to treehouses with a "No Girls Allowed" Sign . . . money symbols, dollars . . . George Washington on a dollar bill, Martha Washington on a fifty-nine-cent piece . . . Washington tosses a dollar across the Delaware, but Martha's got only fifty-nine cents to throw . . . dollars . . . hmm. An office scene. The sign on the wall displays his "First Dollar." Above the secretary next to him is her "First 59¢."

I never know where the train of thought will lead. When Reagan was urging Congress to fund the Contras, he compared those thugs to the founding fathers. Reagan was a buffoon, a cynical clown, and that reminded me of a McDonald's commercial. Maybe Reagan could be Ronald McDonald singing "You deserve a break today" to the Contras . . . Naaah. Then I wondered how the founding fathers would feel about Reagan's comparison. That reminded me of the famous image we all have of the signing of the Declaration of Independence. How would the Contras look sitting there? Then what . . . ? If they were the "moral equivalent of the founding fathers," as Reagan said, then who would be today's redcoats? Civilian women and children? What would be Bunker Hill? A village hospital? Was Reagan the moral equivalent of a president? That was some-

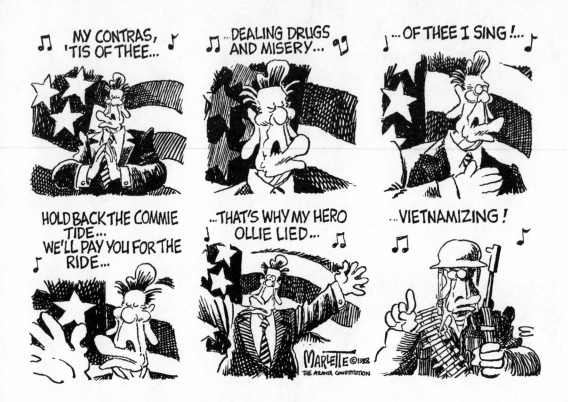

♪♫ MY CONTRAS, 'TIS OF THEE... ♪

♪♫ ...DEALING DRUGS AND MISERY... ♫♫

♪ ...OF THEE I SING !... ♪

HOLD BACK THE COMMIE TIDE... WE'LL PAY YOU FOR THE RIDE... ♪

...THAT'S WHY MY HERO OLLIE LIED... ♫

...VIETNAMIZING ! ♪♫

MARLETTE ©1988
THE ATLANTA CONSTITUTION

thing to work on, but I kept going. What about the word *Contra*? It sounds like *country* . . . my Contras, right or wrong. But wait. What about Reagan warbling, "My Contras, 'tis of thee, dealing drugs and misery, Of thee I sing . . ."?

A cartoon has to do more than take a familiar image, say Snow White, and apply labels to it: Snow White as the president, with the dwarfs as the cabinet or Congress, just doesn't make it somehow. Part of cartooning's art is finding a metaphor that is organically connected to the subject and that sheds light on the topic. This is what separates the heavyweights in cartooning from the wannabees. An example of true inappropriateness would be drawing an exploding Dumbo after the tragic explosion of an Army transport plane. Or using Dennis the Menace with a slingshot to illustrate the conflict between the Palestinian kids and Israeli soldiers. Both of these trivialize poignant situations. Funny drawings are important, but they should always serve an appropriate idea.

Everything and anything goes into the memory hopper for cartoon ideas. The crackdown on the

EVERYTHING GOES INTO THE MEMORY HOPPER

West Bank and the deportation of Palestinians naturally led me to Holy Land images and biblical precedents. I thought of the suffering children of Israel, Moses before Pharoah . . . "Let My People Go" . . . the sacrifice of Isaac by Abraham, the stoning of the prophets . . . the prophet Jeremiah . . . didn't he say some pretty strong stuff about the mistreatment of others? I vaguely recalled from Sunday school a quote from Jeremiah that I might be able to use. I scoured the book of Jeremiah until I found it and used the entire quote in a cartoon.

When Bush swept the South on Super Tuesday I looked for traditional southern images to illustrate the win. The classic movie poster image of Scarlett swooning in Rhett's arms leaped immediately to mind, and it was an easy step to

"GONE WITH THE WIMP"

and alter the legend to read "Gone with the Wimp."

When the Supreme Court made abortions tougher for the poor, I began thinking of limos, yachts, country clubs, furs, jewelry — which reminded me of the phrase "If you have to ask how much, you can't afford one!" I drew a Supreme Court justice at the door of an abortion clinic greeting a poor pregnant woman with that line.

" IF YOU HAVE TO ASK HOW MUCH, YOU CAN'T AFFORD ONE! "

When I wanted to draw something on the reunification of Germany, I immediately thought of coupling images — marriage, dating, and so on. The uniting of the two countries seemed full of so much potential danger that I was reminded of the fears of sexually transmissible diseases, and then of safe sex. That spawned the idea of East and West Germany as a couple in bed, with the motto on the wall, "Practice safe reunification."

Unfortunately, I don't know any one-two-three recipe for coming up with cartoon ideas. As much as we cartoonists try to codify it, ritualize the magic so that it can be summoned easily, the process is still instinctual. Just like writers who have their superstitions — I heard about one writer who couldn't put one word in front of another unless the room was filled with the aroma of rotting apples — we cartoonists have our own creative idiosyncrasies. Some soak in warm baths to get ideas, others stoke up on high-octane coffee. Some schmooze in the newsroom or keep vampire hours. Whatever works.

Some cartoonists sweat each cartoon out of their pores. It involves a lot of grunting and pushing until the drawing is forced out, and usually the strain shows in their work. The best cartoonists develop an easy kind of relationship with their muse. Their cartoons seem effortless, like breathing or the beat of their hearts. Being told that your work is "natural" is the highest compliment a cartoonist can receive. The great ones are natural — like Michael Jordan's jump shot,

Baryshnikov's leap, Itzhak Perlman's violin flourishes, and Navratilova's backhand. Those people make it look easy. Of course, we never see the hours on the court or ballet barre and the years of practice, repetition, and mental and physical challenge — learning the basics, training the brain and body to attend to things that feel unnatural at first.

The way a cartoonist gets ideas is connected to the kind he's after. You hunt a Bengal tiger differently than you hunt a snipe. My tastes run to the great beasts, the wild and scary ideas that dwell in the dangerous terrain of symbols charged with emotion and forbidden associations. If you stalk them where they live, they are more likely to spring from the thickets to surprise you. Finding the ideas that punch my ticket means following the heat of passion through society's totems and taboos. A columnist or editorial writer can say the president is insensitive to the handicapped, but a cartoonist can draw him pushing somebody in a wheelchair down a flight of stairs.

A cartoon I drew for the *Atlanta Constitution* had this quality. The paper was publishing a series on discriminatory loan practices against blacks by local banks. (These stories later won a Pulitzer Prize.) On a story as outrageous as this, a cartoon didn't have to exaggerate much. The contrast between Atlanta's New South idea of itself and the old-fashioned racism the banks were practicing brought obvious images to mind — lynchings, segregationists standing in doorways, "White" and "Colored" signs over toilets and water fountains, robed Klansmen. My cartoon simply showed a black couple facing an Atlanta bank teller who explained, "You'll need to speak to one of our loan officers." The loan officer seated at a nearby desk wore the hooded white sheets of a Ku Klux Klansman.

The banks went berserk. "The stories were bad enough, but that cartoon!" they yelped. The paper's publisher, an extraordinarily soulless, empty suit of a man, who had delayed the story as long as possible, also complained. "The story was solid journalism. Unassailable. But Marlette fixed that!" Suddenly he was supporting work he had been extremely squeamish about — until my cartoon gave him something new to point at. Kovach defended the cartoon by asking the publisher and his banker cronies, "How else would you draw it?"

YOU HUNT A BENGAL TIGER DIFFERENTLY THAN YOU HUNT A SNIPE

That question perfectly defines the kinds of cartoons I'm always after — ones that need no more defense than "How else would you draw it?" One of the most potent ways of getting there is to have a public figure like Saddam Hussein as a target. Hussein was the perfect cartoon villain. His invasion of Kuwait had a lot in common with Hitler's early aggression. I doodled a drawing of Hussein as Hitler . . . Hitler in a burnoose . . . Hitler on a camel. Then I shifted gears . . . Hussein is like a predatory animal . . . sharks, tigers, rats, snakes. How about a snake swallowing a rabbit, Kuwait. Hmm. Predators . . . something mean and ugly, wolves, sharks, spiders . . . Spiders reminded me of the movie *Arachnophobia* . . . Iraqnophobia. Bingo!

One of my favorite kinds of cartoon ideas results from politicians slipping up and showing their true selves, warts and all — Biden's plagiarized speeches, the Reagans as astrology nuts, Gary Hart with his pants down. We love to have the emperor's nakedness show us that our leaders are as human as we are.

Often the politicians themselves are our best gag writers. Ed Meese once said, "I see no evidence of hungry children in America!" It was an easy step to draw Meese with a full belly, oblivious of a starving child holding an empty bowl underneath him.

" I SEE NO EVIDENCE OF HUNGRY CHILDREN IN AMERICA! "

Sometimes cartoon ideas just jump out at you. When Ronald Reagan appointed James Watt as secretary of the Interior, I remember reading about his record as a certifiable anti-environment nut and thinking, "My God! This guy would shoot Bambi!" I drew him with Bambi's head as a trophy on his office wall.

When George Bush was desperately trying to shake his wimp image I drew him trapped in a package of weenies.

Michael Dukakis was such a boring campaigner that I decided to turn the insomnia cliché upside down and draw a sheep counting Dukakises to fall asleep.

Sometimes an idea comes together so easily that I'm immediately suspicious that it's too obvious, that everybody else is going to do the same thing. There's actually a fine line between a flash of insight and the dull sheen of banality. Knowing the difference is part of the job.

I especially look for opportunities to put our leaders into ordinary household situations. One way to demythologize

them is to show them running to the store for milk and bread, taking out the garbage, or watching the tube in bed. When Gorbachev first came to America and charmed the pants off us, I drew the Great Communicator and Nancy in bed watching TV. ". . . and filling in for Johnny this week is *Mikhail Gorbachev.*"

When Bush was obsessing over a flag-burning amendment, I had him sitting at the breakfast table, smoke rising from the toaster. Barbara explains, "No, George, we don't need a constitutional amendment against burning the *toast!*"

"NO, GEORGE — WE DON'T NEED A CONSTITUTIONAL AMENDMENT AGAINST BURNING THE *TOAST!*"

Some people can't imagine drawing a cartoon every day. It would be like writing a high school English theme every day. "You must think about it all the time," they say. "It must dominate your every waking thought! I'd be a nervous wreck!" At first it does take you over, but with time and practice you relax into it and even enjoy the pressure of being out on the high wire every day.

Larry Bird, the Boston Celtics great, once talked about why he was so dependable in the crunch. He explained that lots of players want to be a hero and take the last shot when the score is tied. That's every schoolboy's fantasy. But only a handful want the ball when their team is down a point.

That's when Larry Bird wants the ball; it's the mark of a champion. The key is wanting to be in the tough, challenging spot. It's the same with cartooning. Not every day and not every cartoon, but I've learned to love a blank sheet of paper on deadline. It braces me with its endless potential and possibility. When the game is on the line, put me in, Coach!

"PUT ME IN, COACH!"

US AND THEM

I'M GONNA TAKE MY BALL AND GO HOME!

THE WORLD HAS UNDERGONE a lot of cosmetic surgery since I first started drawing cartoons. The Vietnam war ended, China opened up, Arabs and Israelis got together at Camp David, Gorbachev gave us glasnost (then took it back), the Berlin Wall came down — bringing with it communism in Eastern Europe — Japan and West Germany rose to economic dominance, and Saddam Hussein taught us to give war a chance, and we made him regret it.

Even in the last couple of years we've witnessed some dramatic changes, although it is amazing how much George Bush's New World Order looks like the Old World Disorder. But with all that's happened, it's hard for cartoonists to keep up with who we can dump on nowadays. Former enemies are now friends. Former friends can't be trusted. It's confusing. Once upon a time it was safe to bash the Japanese and the Germans. Now we have to borrow money from them. Everybody we once bombed the hell out of seems to come back and kick our butts economically. Any day now I expect to buy a Vietnamese VCR or fax machine. In forty-five years Americans will be driving Iraqi automobiles.

These cartoons remind us how much has happened around the world in the last twenty years — and how little has changed.

"...WE'RE ALL OUT OF BREAD AND SUGAR... OH, AND WE'RE RUNNING LOW ON ANTI-TANK WEAPONS — SO DON'T FORGET TO PICK UP SOME HOSTAGES!"

CAMP DAVID HUSTLE

"YOUR CHILD WAS KILLED AT MY CHILD'S FUNERAL?... I THOUGHT MY CHILD WAS KILLED AT YOUR CHILD'S FUNERAL!"

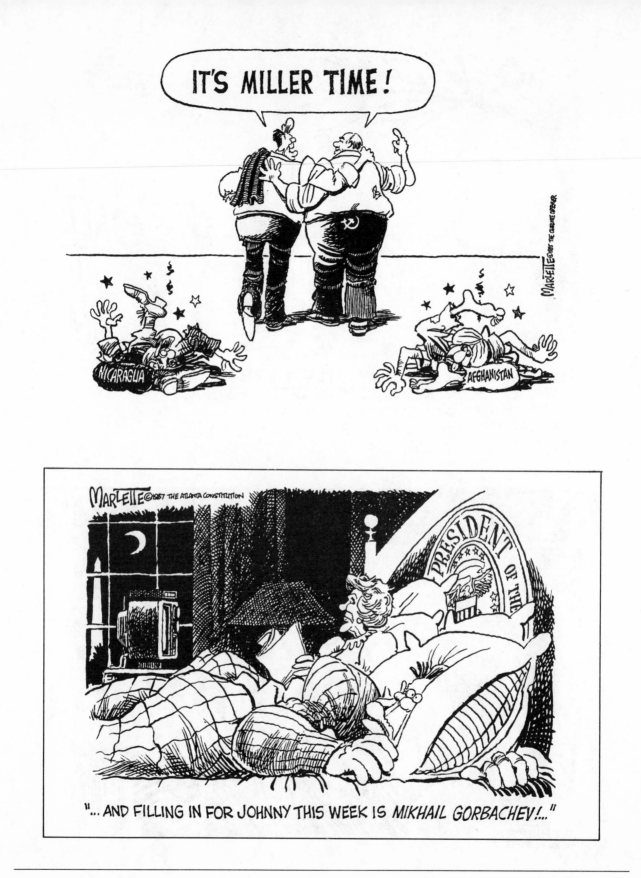

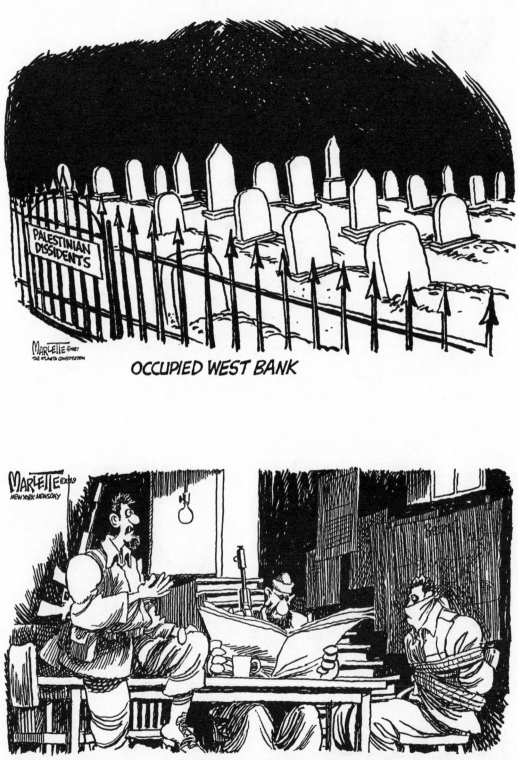

OCCUPIED WEST BANK

"I FORGET— DID WE TAKE A HOSTAGE IN RESPONSE TO AN EXECUTION IN RETALIATION FOR KIDNAPPING A TERRORIST?... OR DID WE KIDNAP A TERRORIST IN RETALIATION FOR TAKING A HOSTAGE IN RESPONSE TO AN EXECUTION?"

"...THIS LAND IS YOUR LAND!...THIS LAND IS MY LAND!... FROM CALIFORNIA... TO THE NEW YORK ISLANDS!..."

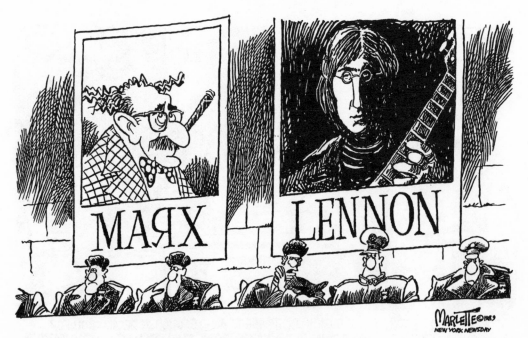

" GORBACHEV'S GOING TOO FAST! "

"CONFIDENTIALLY, DON'T YOU JUST *HATE* IT WHEN THE WORKERS OF THE WORLD UNITE?"

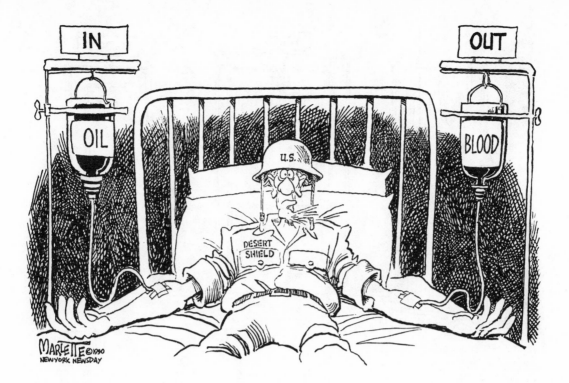

" I MISS THE AYATOLLAH! "

"YOUR FATHER'S A BABY-BOOM LIBERAL, DEAR—HE'S NEVER HAD A WAR HE COULD SUPPORT BEFORE!"

WHEN
CARTOONISTS
BOND

A CARTOONISTS' CONVENTION? What fun!" Wild and crazy, madcap zanies running around with arrows through their heads, wearing Slinky glasses and bunny ears, squirting seltzer bottles, throwing cream pies, exchanging witty repartee, playing practical jokes on each other until somebody calls the cops. Well, not quite.

Cartoonists' conventions are pretty much like the gatherings of any other professionals — except auto parts salesmen and Shriners don't draw on their tablecloths. Our conventions are like cartoons of other conventions: we drink, talk shop, drink, meet, drink, take bus trips, drink, hear guest speakers, drink, participate in panel discussions, and drink. Nothing is more inspiring for a young cartoonist than finding out that the person whose work you admire the most is a drunk.

When cartoonist Mike Peters was flying to London for his first convention, he was seated next to veteran Wayne Stayskal. Mike asked him who was on the plane, and Stayskal rolled off a litany of greats. Soon they saw a man crawling down the aisle chasing an ice cube that had fallen out of his glass.

"And that's Bill So and So," said Stayskal.

"Oh wow," enthused Mike, "I have a book of his cartoons." Even on his hands and knees, the gray eminence lost none of his stature in the young rookie's eyes.

As the gentleman approached, Stayskal leaned across Peters's aisle seat and tapped the man on the shoulder. "Bill, I'd like you to meet Mike Peters," he said.

The crawling cartoonist looked up, bleary-eyed and red-faced. "Hiya, kid!" he said, tousling Mike's

"HIYA, KID!"

hair, and continued down the aisle. So much for heroes.

There are two major cartoonists' organizations. The National Cartoonists Society is made up of doodlers of every stripe, from comic strippers to animators to editorial cartoonists to advertising artists to magazine gagsters; members of the Association of American Editorial Cartoonists are political cartoonists only. They both hold conventions, and the NCS gives an annual Reuben Award, our equivalent of the Oscar, named for the great and wildly inventive cartoonist Rube Goldberg.

The idea that we get together at all is amusing to me. "Cartoonists' organization" seems like a real oxymoron — like "working press" or "military intelligence." Parliamentary procedure and Robert's Rules of Order give most cartoonists hives. Still, it's a lonesome profession — only a few hundred of us drawing in this country — so what's a few business meetings and bylaws if we get to booze and schmooze together once a year.

I'll never forget my first convention. It was June 17, a Saturday night in 1972, an election year. As I was doodling on my menu at the Statler-Hilton Hotel in Washington, D.C., listening to Attorney General Richard Kleindienst extol the Nixon administration's dedication to law and order, burglars were breaking into the Democratic National Committee headquarters at the Watergate complex. The following morning we read a small item about the break-in in the *Washington Post*. The coverup had begun, and we cartoonists were dying to get to our drawing boards. We all discussed the story, and before long we were tossing around ideas that practically placed Nixon at the scene of the crime. I was twenty-two years old, and little did I know we would all soon help topple the government.

Somehow it seemed right that my first cartoonists' convention ushered in Watergate. Satirists see national political disasters the way a cosmetic surgeon looks at cellulite (it may be ugly, but hey! . . . it's a living!), and Watergate was one of the richest gold mines in cartooning history. I was still in my gee-whiz phase then, not quite believing how fortunate I was to have landed a job doing what I loved at the *Charlotte Observer*. I was also meeting the faces behind the signatures I had studied so lovingly for so long — Bill Sanders, Hugh Haynie, the great Canadian artist Duncan MacPherson.

THE REUBEN AWARD

Herblock even came down from Parnassus to stroll among the mortals.

I also met some of my contemporaries just starting out: Mike Peters, Jeff MacNelly, and Tony Auth. We talked shop in the hotel bar, clutching our drawings, shyly but proudly showing them around and oohing and aahing over each other's work. This was before any of us were widely syndicated, so it was the first time we had seen the work of our peers. While we took measure of each other we also took sustenance. It was intoxicating.

At that convention my preconceived notions about my chosen profession and those who practiced it ran headlong into reality. Most people think cartoonists are all liberals, because most of the greats are, but I discovered at a briefing by press secretary Ron Ziegler that a great majority of America's cartoonists are quite conservative.

Ziegler gave us his usual gloss and flatulence, but surprisingly no one either questioned or challenged him. In fact, these professional rock throwers were actually solicitous. Puzzled though I was, I deferred to my elders and kept my silence. When in Rome, do as the Romans, and obviously they don't question Caesar or his flacks.

Later, Commerce Secretary Pete Peterson gave a speech defending Nixon's wage-price tamperings, and the reaction was the same. That is, until Tony Auth of the *Philadelphia Inquirer* jokingly asked Peterson, "Are you a socialist?" While the secretary was feebly stammering denials, the rest of the room was in shock, harrumphing and raising their eyebrows.

That was the first crack in our group decorum, but when

the hawkish senator from Boeing, Henry "Scoop" Jackson, addressed us, things totally unraveled. This was about the time when Nixon's promise of peace was turning into Vietnamization. Fewer Americans were dying, but more Southeast Asians were being killed, and the bombings had been stepped up, widening the war into Laos and Cambodia. Jackson had handed out a copy of his speech beforehand. He knew he was addressing a group of cartoonists and had laced the speech with lines that must have been humorous to him. Unfortunately, they weren't funny on paper and were even less so when uttered out loud. About halfway through, Jackson noticed he was bombing, so to speak, and shifted gears into commie-bashing oratory — the kind that probably killed 'em at the defense contractor testimonials and Kiwanis meetings back in Spokane.

I listened to his Cold War simplicities, thinking, "Okay! this is it! We're going to eat him alive. There'll be a feeding frenzy when he finishes." When Scoop asked for questions, a hand shot up. "Senator, what can we do as cartoonists to stop the communist threat?" I couldn't believe it. After a couple more softballs from the crowd, I was fuming. They were letting him get away with this.

"Senator" — I had raised my hand and was talking — "if it's true that peace comes from strength, as you stated, can you explain why the United States, the strongest nation in the world, has been waging war on Vietnam, one of the weakest nations in the world, for the last ten years or so with your help in the U.S. Senate?"

A gasp rose from the audience. I had breached the etiquette. Heads were craning to see who had been so impertinent. Jackson squared off and shot back something about my question being just the kind of fuzzy-headed thinking he expected from the media. We were off to the races. He sputtered something about what it was like being at war and how we never could have beaten Hitler with my kind of thinking. Bill Sanders of the *Milwaukee Journal* stood up and shouted, "Are you comparing Ho Chi Minh to Adolph Hitler?" Then Tony Auth joined in: "Senator, there are many thoughtful Americans who disagree on the war . . ." Pretty soon a lively back and forth was going, and I asked more questions, provoking Jackson to sputter and shout so much that the vein in his forehead was poking out. The cartoonists were riveted.

Afterward one of the wives congratulated me for starting an actual debate for a change, but a couple of older Cold War cartoonists told me I had been disrespectful to a United States senator. "After all," one said, "he has more information than you." I was learning that a lot of political cartoonists, like some journalists, are secretly dazzled and intimidated by the famous. It is distressing to watch these professionals kiss up to every politician who deigns to address them. The puckering grows especially wet and sloppy for presidents. Some cartoonists will give away their drawing hand for any opportunity to bask in the presence of a commander-in-chief — whether he's in office or out.

LAPDOG CARTOONIST

Lyndon Johnson loved cartoons and collected originals for his presidential library. When the cartoonists held their convention in Austin, Johnson took a couple of busloads on an impromptu tour of his ranch. He tore off across the rugged terrain in his Lincoln Continental convertible, giving a running commentary on the passing scenery over a public address system hooked up to the buses. Every so often he screeched his automobile to a stop, jumped out, and poured poison on one of the red ant hills infesting the ranch. Soon one of the cartoonists at the back of a bus began chanting, "Hey, hey, LBJ, how many ants have you killed today?!"

Nixon's affection for cartoonists was more reserved, since he had been our prize target for years. We never made his A-list, though Herblock and Paul Conrad made his famous Enemies List. Jerry Ford invited us to a White House reception once, and after he retired he held a gathering in Grand Rapids for the humorists and cartoonists who had skewered him and his bumbling over the years. Jimmy Carter, unfortunately, was too self-serious and shy to hit it off much with cartoonists.

Ronald Reagan's public admission that the comics are the first thing he reads in the morning made most of the nation groan, but cartoonists saw their opening. Soon a group of editorial cartoonists wrangled an invitation to the White House, followed by a photo op and press gathering in the Rose Garden. While Reagan genially joked about his favorite comics and his famous notebook doodles, ABC's Sam Donaldson shouted, "Mr. President, did you approve selling arms to the Ayatollah Khomeini to raise funds for the Contras?" For a minute Reagan was caught off guard — it looked like he might have to answer without a script or prompting by his wife. As he squirmed, fumbling for words, a voice suddenly rose from the revealers of imperial nudity themselves, the cartoonists: "Mr. President, I move we adjourn this meeting!"

Reagan brightened and gratefully agreed. "Well, I second that motion." The stunned gathering quickly broke up, and a relieved Reagan escaped into the wings.

Over the years and some pretty grueling bus trips we conventioneers have seen a number of celebs, politicos, and the homes of the rich and not always famous. In Boston we were carted to the Kennedy compound in Hyannisport; in Nashville we were bused to Opryland and to a barbecue at the home of country singer-songwriter Tom T. Hall. In Milwaukee we saw the breweries, and in Oklahoma City . . . don't ask.

If a convention speaker sticks in my head, it's almost always because of the cutting up we did during the talk. Although Gene McCarthy was wittier than most, all during his speech Jeff MacNelly and I wrote verses to a folk song on our menus, to the tune of "John Henry." We called it "The Ballad of Thomas Nast" — "Tom Nast was a ink-slingin' man, Lawd, Lawd, Tom Nast was a ink-slingin' man."

Ralph Nader couldn't resist trying to reform the cartoonists. In his dour, sermonizing way, he challenged us to police ourselves. He suggested we raise our professional standards by having ethics committees, mandatory public policy seminars, and even training camps, a kind of minor league farm system for young cartoonists. MacNelly passed me a drawing he'd scrawled on his menu. It featured a caricature of me in baseball cap and sweats with the words "Marlette's Kartoon Kamp for Kids" emblazoned on my chest. I was blowing a whistle at a cluster of miniature drawing boards and yelling with a drill instructor's impatience, "Tweep! Okay, kids, time to work on Nixon's nose!"

JEFF MACNELLY'S SKETCH

All this sketching during meals or cocktail parties, panel discussions or speeches gets the competitive juices flowing and inevitably leads to spirited sessions of one-upmanship. We try to top each other with cartoon "takes" that supply visual footnotes to every conversation. And almost everyone caricatures the speaker, especially if it's a famous senator or cabinet member or, better still, the president. Afterward some of the groupie-type cartoonists rush up to the front and get their work autographed so they can impress their Rotary Club friends back in Sheepdip, Iowa, or Dogsqueeze, Georgia. For years these drawings would be of the president, say, with his hands on the helm of the Ship of State and a heroic Uncle Sam nearby, saying, "Steady as she goes!" or "That's my boy!" Or maybe the American eagle with its wing around the president, saying, "Well done!" But my generation changed all that.

In Quebec City, while the head of the Royal Canadian Mounted Police delivered his after-dinner lecture, Arnold Roth drew various Mounties and their horses mounting the Queen of England and having their wanton way with her.

Later, as the mayor gave an endless, boring speech that wouldn't die, Tony Auth drew the banquet room with all of us asleep and the sun coming up outside while the mayor droned on. This sketch was a departure for Tony, who was then deep into his anatomically correct frog period — a wonderful stage of his artistic development when most of the doodles featured frogs with gargantuan penises.

We definitely take advantage of these conventions to cast aside whatever restraints and inhibitions we feel working for family newspapers. Once in Boston, Vice President Jerry Ford spoke to us just a few months before Nixon's resignation. Mike Peters drew Ford as a dirty old man, opening his overcoat to expose genitalia that bore a striking resemblance to Richard Nixon — think of the nose and an especially hairy five o'clock shadow covering his bulbous jowls. I drew a GOP elephant walking away from a pile of elephant poop that looked an awful lot like the vice president. Sophomoric but effective.

We rarely show these scatological drawings to the guests of honor. The closest we ever came was after Ford's speech, when I convinced Tony Auth to ask the vice president to autograph his. Ford was dutifully signing the usual flattering portraits of himself astride the American eagle, when suddenly the wild-eyed, bearded Auth stood before him, looking for all the world like an assassin. Auth held out a caricature of Jerry Ford as a snake, forked tongue and all. Ford looked at the drawing, back up at the grinning Auth, then back at the drawing. When the Secret Service saw the sketch, they nearly pulled their revolvers and wrestled it to the floor. But Ford glanced questioningly at Auth. "Just put 'To my friend Tony, from Jerry Ford,'" Auth suggested. And that's exactly

MIKE PETERS'S SKETCH

what
Ford
wrote!

What a coup!
Tony had his
own original
drawing of soon-
to-be-president Ford
as a snake in the grass,
autographed by the serpent himself, to
hang proudly in his bathroom at home.

Almost twenty years ago the late Howard Simons, who was then managing editor of the *Washington Post,* hosted a sort of mini-convention dinner for a few of us — Tony Auth, Jeff MacNelly, Mike Peters, and I were charter invitees — which has since grown into an annual bash held in the *Post*'s Executive Dining Room for a number of cartoonists. The guests include those regularly reprinted in the *Post*'s Saturday Drawing Board roundup of cartoons as well as *Post* cartoonist Herblock, Mrs. Katherine Graham, publisher Don Graham, Haynes Johnson, David Broder, various special guests such as Bob Woodward or Ted Koppel, and usually a senator, presidential candidate, or cabinet official. Now the dinner is hosted by the editorial page editor, Meg Greenfield, who inherited it when Howard took over the Nieman curatorship at Harvard.

The evening usually turns into a round-table swap of anecdotes, impressions, stories, even home videos, and ends with some wacky road trip into the wilds of official Washington. On Lincoln's birthday one year we all drove to the great president's memorial at two in the morning and stood on the steps singing a loud, drunken rendition of "Happy

Birthday" to Honest Abe. Once, when Senator Pat Moynihan was showing us the famous Senate Watergate hearing room, Mike Peters jumped into an old-time wooden phone booth and came out in the Superman costume his wife had made for him to wear trick or treating with their kids. Some of us hid Peters's clothes, so he had to wander the halls of the Capitol in his Man of Steel getup, to the bewilderment of the night watchmen and cleaning ladies. At the following year's *Post* dinner, after Herblock won his third Pulitzer, Mike gave him the Superman costume.

Howard Simons set a rule that no one outside the cartoonist circle could attend two years in a row, but Pat Moynihan got around this by showing up in black tie as a waiter. We were well into the second course before any of us recognized that the man refilling our wine glasses was the senior senator from New York, wearing a hairnet.

There's lots of faux pas potential at these do's. One cartoonist's wife, excitedly talking about getting her pilot's license, asked Senator John (Right Stuff) Glenn, the first man to circle the planet in a spacecraft, if he was instrument-certified. Another night Joe Califano graciously invited us to see his new office. One of the spouses christened it by tossing her cookies all over the new carpet of the secretary of health, education and welfare.

We've also discovered some amazing talents from surprising sources. Ted Koppel, Mr. Serious Newscaster, writes very witty parodies pegged to news events (to the tune of the Dr. Pepper jingle, he sang, "I'm a Contra, You're a Contra"). Mark Alan ("Washingtoon") Stamaty does some exotic impressions, including an unforgettable Elvis. He usually closes the evening with his rendition of "You Ain't Nothin' But a Hound Dog."

This is all great fun, but there is an underside to cartoonist bonding. At a recent NCS gathering we proved that women's liberation never laid a hand on us. Over the years our ranks have been spiced up by successful women cartoonists, such as Claire Bretecher, Lynda Barry, Lynn Johnston, and Cathy Guisewite, as well as editorial cartoonists, including Etta Hulme, M. G. Lord, Kate Salley Palmer, and Signe Wilkinson, a recent Pulitzer finalist. But the profession is still predominantly male, and because of our Old Boy biases, a program intended to salute Our Gal Cartoonists ended up patronizing them instead. The honorees paraded on stage with Miss America sashes that read "Lady Cartoonist," accompanied by lame, often sex-stereotyped, commentary.

Another expression of our dark side is Pen-point Envy. Professional jealousy enjoys a long and rich tradition among cartoonists. Probably one of the reasons we get so mightily crocked when we're together is to anesthetize ourselves from those feelings. It's the only way we can gloss over and protect ourselves from the jealous rages we sometimes feel toward each other.

The doodles-and-chuckles racket has always had its battles among the rank and file, with wannabees jockeying for position among the cartoon gods and established deities defending their turf. Plagiarism charges fly constantly. Cartoonists regularly accuse one another of stealing ideas or drawing styles, but the accused are usually guilty just of stealing thunder. Predictably, the ones most vocal about plagiarism often turn out to be the worst offenders.

Ham ("Joe Palooka") Fisher once accused his former assistant, Al ("Li'l Abner") Capp, of drawing hidden pornography in his strip and called for a Senate investigation. Fisher was ultimately drummed out of the National Cartoonists Society for making the accusation. Another famous comic strip artist took a rising young rival for a spin in his sports car. At first the young admirer was flattered and thrilled to be riding with his idol, until he noticed that the gas pedal was pushed to the floor, and they were speeding faster and faster . . . sixty, seventy . . . eighty . . . ninety miles per hour — until the older artist intentionally drove the car straight into a tree. Miraculously, they both survived, but the driver later died, apparently a suicide, when he drove his sports car into a tree.

One editorial cartoonist refused to allow a news magazine to reprint his work when they put a rival on their cover instead of him. If Pen-point Envy is left unchecked, it grows into Pulitzer Lust, which can lead to the deadly Awards Deficiency Syndrome. Editorial cartoonists are leading carri-

ers of Pulitzer Lust and, thus, a high-risk group for ADS. The only thing worse than seeing another editorial cartoonist get "the Prize," as some cartoonists reverentially refer to it, is having it go to a comic stripper. When Garry ("Doonesbury") Trudeau won it, some editorial cartoonists fired off a protest to the Pulitzer advisory board, and Berke ("Bloom County") Breathed's prize nearly caused them to riot and burn down the Pulitzer headquarters at Columbia University.

But all in all, cartoonists get along together about as well as most professional groups, maybe better than some — as long as the booze is flowing and nobody pulls out a tape measure and starts measuring the others' pen points.

ACKNOWLEDGMENTS

First I want to sing the praises of my wife, Melinda, who suggested the idea for this book.

I am also grateful to my agent, Esther Newberg, who "got" the book right away and had the instincts, the good sense, and the savvy to understand that Houghton Mifflin should publish it and that Henry Ferris should be its editor. I want to thank Henry Ferris, who is much too young to be such a great editor, for his intelligence, patience, and good humor and for the clarity and steadfastness of his vision.

I want to thank all of the *Charlotte Observer* editors who saw fit early on to open their pages to my kind of commentary: C. A. McKnight, Reese Cleghorn, Jim Batten, David Lawrence, Ed Williams, Jerry Shinn, and Rich Oppel.

I am especially grateful to Bill Kovach, a great editor and a journalist's journalist, a true believer in free speech, who not only talks the talk but walks the walk, for letting me be a part of his grand and glorious vision in Atlanta. Also I thank the gallant Dudley Clendinen, who shared the dream, and Wendell Rawls, the last of the Spartan warriors, for his friendship and support when it counted.

I want to thank *Newsday* publisher Robert Johnson, editor Tony Marro, and editorial page editor Jim Klurfeld, and Tom Plate, now editorial page editor at the *Los Angeles Times,* who brought me to The Show to practice my craft. And thanks to *New York Newsday* editorial page editor Ernest Tollerson for his friendship, support, and unfailing wisdom. Thanks also to Claudette Leandro, poet and editorial assistant, a rare and delightful combo.

I can only rhapsodize about my great good friend, fellow

ambivalent southerner, brilliant novelist, sometime collaborator, and unindicted co-conspirator, Pat Conroy, with love and gratitude for our ongoing dialogue and his encouragement of my halting steps out of the primordial ooze of dreams and images and onto the higher ground of language, into the civilization of words. Thanks also to Lenore Conroy for her friendship, love, and generosity of spirit.

I hoist a glass to my cartoonist friends and their spouses: Jeff MacNelly, Tony Auth, Mike and Marian Peters, Jules Feiffer and Jennifer Allen, Arnold and Caroline Roth, and Mell Lazarus for their various drawings, memories, and inadvertent contributions to this manuscript as well as their ongoing friendship and inspiration.

To Rick Newcombe, Anita Medeiros, and all the folks at Creators Syndicate for their unfailing enthusiasm and professionalism.

I want to thank Anne Chalmers for her unerring graphic instincts in the design of this book, and Peg Anderson, my manuscript editor, for her excellent eye and ear. And thanks to Holley Bishop, Sara Eisenman, Lori Glazer, Nancy Grant, John Sterling, and all the gang at Houghton Mifflin for making this an unabashed publishing pleasure for me from start to finish.

And finally, I want to thank my parents, Elmer Monroe Marlette and Billie Moore Marlette, for their love, for giving me the okay to try, and for not squelching the fire.